KIDNAPPING
THE ILLUSTRATED HISTORY

KIDNAPPING
THE ILLUSTRATED HISTORY

BY HANK MESSICK & BURT GOLDBLATT

1974
THE DIAL PRESS NEW YORK

7-27-82

Manufactured in the United States of America

First printing

Library of Congress Cataloging in Publication Data

Messick, Hank.
   Kidnapping.

   1. Kidnapping—United States—History.   2. Kidnapping—History
   I. Goldblatt, Burt, joint author.   II. Title.
HV6598.M47   364.1'54   74–11245
ISBN 0–8037–4433–1

In memory of two beautiful people—
Irwin and Margot Weinbaum

CONTENTS

Fat men don't get kidnapped; they don't fit into car trunks very well.

Reg Murphy, 1974

INTRODUCTION

February 4, 1974, and a beautiful coed-heiress is carried half naked through the broken glass door of a Berkeley, California, town house and dumped into the trunk of a waiting car. A fusillade of covering rifle fire shatters the silence and the car carrying Patricia Campbell Hearst roars away into the night.

February 20, 1974, and a Georgia newspaper editor is riding with a stranger along Interstate 85 near Atlanta. Suddenly the stranger produces a nickel-plated revolver and announces: "Mr. Murphy, you have been kidnapped." The editor is bound, his eyes taped, and he is shoved into the trunk of the car where a pillow and blanket wait.

March 20, 1974, and a white Ford sedan cuts in front of a limousine carrying Princess Anne of England down the Mall toward Buckingham Palace some two hundred yards away. Both cars stop. From the Ford leaps a little man in a raincoat. He fires a volley of shots at the royal vehicle. A bullet narrowly misses the Princess who huddles with her new husband in a corner of the car. The gunman gives up and flees. In his abandoned car is found a ransom note demanding more than four million dollars for Anne's safe return.

Sensational cases all three, and naturals for headlines around the world. Even in a period marked by top-level changes of government in England and Israel, the death of a president in France, and the continuing drive to impeach the President of the United States, these kidnappings got major coverage in the media. Perhaps inevitably, the publicity generated other kidnap efforts, and suddenly there was crisis. Kidnap insurance policies were advertised, private security agencies reported a dramatic increase in the demand for bodyguards, and, predictably, President Richard M. Nixon ordered Attorney General William Saxbe to press for reinstitution of the death penalty in cases where a kidnap victim is killed.

Kidnapping first became a capital crime in the United States following the murder of Charles A. Lindbergh, Jr., in 1932. Called "the crime of the century," the Lindbergh tragedy spawned a cycle of kidnappings that lasted several years. When it ended, some observers with more faith than facts credited the "Lindbergh Law" with making the crime unpopular. The FBI got a lot of the glory as well. Indeed, many years later Herbert Hoover looked back and wrote: "The efficiency and courage of the FBI under J. Edgar Hoover finally stamped out this particular crime wave. The fears in the hearts of millions of mothers were lifted."

All of which was, of course, nonsense. Kidnappings continued through the years after the Lindbergh case just as they had occurred in the years before. With a few notable exceptions they got little attention. The FBI, in fact, did not bother to keep accurate records—perhaps lest the facts injure the legend. Nevertheless, the kidnappings of the 1930's came at a time of moral as well as economic depression, when people had lost faith in the old standards and were confused and frightened. President Franklin Roosevelt, taking over from Herbert Hoover, found it necessary to assure the nation, "There is nothing to fear but fear itself." But people did fear, and some of them in envy and anger struck at the fortunate who had money by stealing one object beyond price—a human being.

When the 1974 kidnappings occurred, conditions were in some respects better than in 1932, but in one respect they were worse. The government might have failed under President Hoover, but most people then charged nothing more sinister than incompetence. Under President Nixon, however, there was evidence that government had betrayed the people by corrupting the most basic of all democratic processes—the election. Public cynicism developed rapidly until it matched the mood of the Depression years.

Consider these FBI statistics: in the four years between 1969 through 1972, federal kidnap convictions averaged forty-six per year. In 1973—the year the Watergate scandal broke open—there were seventy-one such convictions.

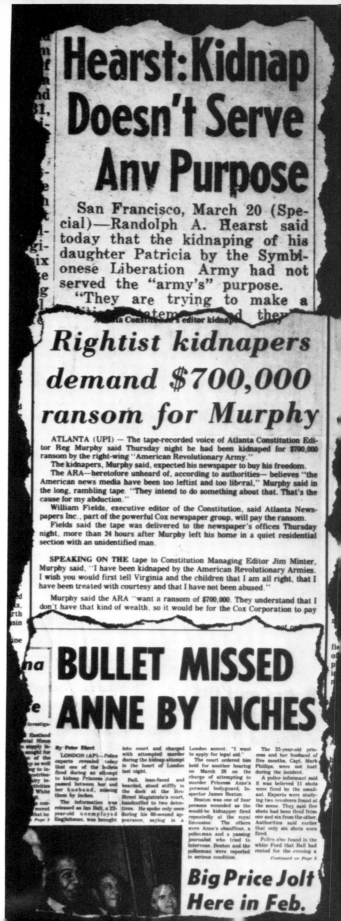

Hearst:Kidnap Doesn't Serve Anv Purpose

San Francisco, March 20 (Special)—Randolph A. Hearst said today that the kidnaping of his daughter Patricia by the Symbionese Liberation Army had not served the "army's" purpose.

"They are trying to make a

Rightist kidnapers demand $700,000 ransom for Murphy

ATLANTA (UPI) — The tape-recorded voice of Atlanta Constitution Editor Reg Murphy said Thursday night he had been kidnaped for $700,000 ransom by the right-wing "American Revolutionary Army."

The kidnapers, Murphy said, expected his newspaper to buy his freedom.

The ARA—heretofore unheard of, according to authorities— believes "the American news media have been too leftist and too liberal," Murphy said in the long, rambling tape. "They intend to do something about that. That's the cause for my abduction."

William Fields, executive editor of the Constitution, said Atlanta Newspapers Inc., part of the powerful Cox newspaper group, will pay the ransom.

Fields said the tape was delivered to the newspaper's offices Thursday night, more than 24 hours after Murphy left his home in a quiet residential section with an unidentified man.

SPEAKING ON THE tape to Constitution Managing Editor Jim Minter, Murphy said, "I have been kidnaped by the American Revolutionary Armies. I wish you would first tell Virginia and the children that I am all right, that I have been treated with courtesy and that I have not been abused."

Murphy said the ARA "want a ransom of $700,000. They understand that I don't have that kind of wealth, so it would be for the Cox Corporation to pay

BULLET MISSED ANNE BY INCHES

By Peter Ebert

LONDON (AP)—Police experts revealed today that one of the bullets fired during an attempt to kidnap Princess Anne passed between her and her husband, missing them by inches.

The information was released as Ian Ball, a 23-year-old unemployed Englishman, was brought into court and charged with attempted murder during the kidnap attempt fired during the incident in the heart of London last night.

Ball, lean-faced and bearded, stood stiffly in the dock at the Bow Street Magistrate's court, handcuffed to two detectives. He spoke only once during his 60-second appearance, saying in a London accent: "I want to apply for legal aid."

The court ordered him held for another hearing on March 28 on the charge of attempting to murder Princess Anne's personal bodyguard, Inspector James Beaton.

Beaton was one of four persons wounded as the would-be kidnaper fired repeatedly at the royal limousine. The others were Anne's chauffeur, a policeman and a passing journalist who tried to intervene. Beaton and the policeman were reported in serious condition.

The 23-year-old princess and her husband of five months, Capt. Mark Phillips, were not hurt during the incident.

A police informant said it was believed 11 shots were fired by the assailant. Experts were studying two revolvers found at the scene. They said five shots had been fired from one and six from the other. Authorities said earlier that only six shots were fired.

Police also found in the white Ford that Ball had rented for the evening a

Continued on Page 3

Big Price Jolt Here in Feb.

Martin Van Buren, who as Governor of New York passed one of the first pieces of legislation dealing with kidnapping in 1829.

In Assembly,

March 3, 1829.

MESSAGE
From his Excellency the Governor.

TO THE SENATE AND ASSEMBLY.

GENTLEMEN—

In the communication which I had the honor to make to the legislature, at the commencement of the session, I apprised you that the act authorising the employment of counsel to assist in the prosecution against persons charged with the abduction of William Morgan, would expire in the month of May next. I have since appointed John C. Spencer, Esq. to be such counsel, in the place of Daniel Mosely, Esq. who has resigned the same, in consequence of his appointment as Circuit Judge. In a letter from Mr. Spencer, addressed to a member of the Senate, and communicated to me, he recommends a continuance of the act for another year; expresses his opinion that no alteration in it is expedient or necessary, and adds that the continuing it in force ought to be disconnected with any provision or proposition whatever. In a more recent letter received from him by me, he repeats his convictions of the urgent necessity that the act should be kept in force for at least one year longer, and requests me [to] recommend the subject to your attention.

No. 132.

2

Believing the original measure to be a very proper one, and concurring fully in the views expressed by the special attorney, I take the liberty of soliciting your early and favorable attention to the subject.

M. V. BUREN.

Albany, March 3d, 1829.

KIDNAP INSURANCE AVAILABLE

Now for the man who appears to have everything, a new kind of insurance has come into prominence, instigated because of the current rash of kidnappings. Not just millionaires, but small business owners, bankers, professional people, corporate officers and their firms are all concerned with how they would be able to cope with the dreadful actuality of a kidnapping and subsequent ransom or extortion demands.

The answer, according to William T. Shilson of American Underwriters Corporation, a Detroit based specialty insurance intermediary, is Kidnapping and Ransom Insurance. The new insurance was created in response to the demand for financial protection from these untimely and increasingly frequent risks.

While Kidnapping and Ransom Insurance policies vary, most contain provisions that the contract remain absolutely secret. In some cases, corporate officials are insured without ever being told; since a leak, however innocent, might encourage kidnapping of the insured individual.

Other provisions of the contract are that the F.B.I. and other law enforcement agencies must be notified of the kidnapping immediately. That all reasonable efforts be made to secure the return of the kidnapped person in some way other than by paying ransom. And that ransom must be paid only under duress. Benefits of the insurance are obvious. Even great wealth is no match for unreasonable demands. And, for the person of modest means, such demands could spell financial disaster.

Says Mr. Shilson, "We are scrupulously careful to protect the identity of our insured." He noted that all requests for information on the new insurance will be handled promptly. Persons interested in this special insurance should contact their agent. The agent can obtain coverage through American Underwriters Corporation, 16311 Mack Avenue, Detroit, Michigan 48224. Phone (313) 886-5300.

Much attention was focused on the ad (left) that appeared in some wealthy suburban newspapers of Detroit, Michigan, recently. But it was nothing new. The news article dates from 1933.

INSURANCE OFFERED AGAINST KIDNAPING

Lloyds Group of London Reported Issuing Policies Up to $100,000.

By the Associated Press.

CHICAGO, Aug. 5 — Insurance against kidnaping up to $100,000 is being offered through a London group (Lloyd's), the Tribune says.

Prominent and wealthy persons in various cities have been secretly insured against the menace under premiums of three-quarters of one per cent for adults and one and a half per cent for children. Because of the greater risk in the case of children the maximum principal amount in such anti-kidnap policies is limited to $50,000, the newspaper said.

Adults also may insure themselves in the same policy against injuries while in the hands of abductors for additional premium payments.

The paper said negotiations for the policies are conducted under conditions of utmost secrecy. Only persons of unquestioned reputation are considered by the insurers and they must have been free from any involvements with shady or undesirable characters. The name of the seeker for insurance is cabled London by code and only the senior

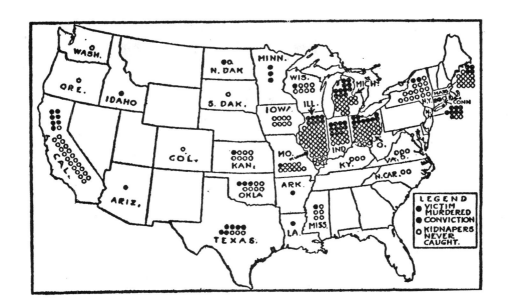

The map (top) shows the extent of kidnapping in 1931. Note the number of kidnappers never caught.
(Below) A 1933 editorial cartoon that would aptly apply to today.

TIME THIS BUSINESS WAS REGULATED.

This was not only almost twice the four-year average but it was 73 per cent higher than the year before. Small wonder then that 1974 should be a climactic year for both Watergate-related cynicism *and* kidnapping.

The crime of kidnapping is not, of course, unique in its relation to the state of public confidence. All crime went up sharply in 1973, the FBI reported, reversing the downward trend of the year before.

While kidnapping is as old as man, the word "kidnap" dates back only to the seventeenth century. Abduction was the word used to mean the physical seizure of women against their will—always a popular practice. When, however, it began to be profitable to steal men and boys to man the ships of the fleet or to serve in the colonies as servants, a new word was coined. "Nap" in those days was a variation of "nab" and was linked with "kid" to mean roughly, "nab the kid."

When under Queen Victoria, the English got around to codifying their laws, they made the kidnapping of children a felony carrying a maximum sentence of seven years. Compare that, however, to the penalty for kidnapping an heiress having an interest "in any real or personal Estate." Fourteen years was the price of such a crime. The severity of the law was based on the Victorian regard for property rights. The law assumed the heiress was not kidnapped for ransom but rather "with intent to marry or carnally know her" in order to achieve a claim upon her estate. Such informal practices were considered downright sneaky, regardless of what the young lady may have thought privately of them.

Today, of course, kidnapping in the sense generally accepted consists of two crimes, abduction and extortion. Associated crimes may include murder if the kidnapper is frightened or sadistic. Money, or as the English put it, "lucre," remains the usual motive, but in recent years the "political kidnapping" has become increasingly important. While relatively new to the United States, it is an old story in other countries and other civilizations.

If a book such as this has any lasting value, it is perhaps in the opportunity it presents to illustrate once again that "crime is a kind of human behavior." There is no panacea; neither new laws nor executive action will bring instant relief. Controlling crime, said the President's Commission on Law Enforcement in 1967, "means changing the hearts and minds of men."

A slow process, certainly.

1. A CRIME FOR ALL SEASONS

We begin with Joseph, the youth of the many-colored coat.

Joseph, so we are told in Genesis, was a fair lad of seventeen but inclined perhaps to be a bit boastful. Secure in his father's favor, he enjoyed dreams of future power and glory which he felt compelled to share with his brothers. His brothers were at once jealous and fearful. Ultimately they conspired to kidnap their brother and to kill him, planning to blame his death on wild animals. In a sense it was a political kidnapping—Joseph threatened to achieve power over them and their tribe— but soon the possibilities of immediate financial gain offered by the kidnapping were recognized. As Judah reasoned:

"What profit is it that we slay our brother and conceal his blood? Come, let us sell him to the Ishmaelites."

So Joseph was hoisted from the dry pit into which he had been flung and was sold into slavery for twenty pieces of silver. He was taken to Egypt and thrown into prison. In Egypt he refused to lie with his master's wife. A virtuous youth, Joseph. Ultimately, virtue would achieve its reward and the dreams of Joseph would come true, but meanwhile his father wept for him as the parents of countless kidnap victims have wept since for missing children.

In the centuries that followed, the institution of slavery became part of the social and economic systems of many nations. The key to slavery was, of course, a continuing supply of able bodies—men, women, and children. Wars supplied some of the demand, but without the organized business of kidnapping—for regardless of its name that's what it was— slavery would have faded. The role of the slave trade in the history of the United States is recent enough to need no discussion here. Let us instead turn to a specific example of kidnapping which gave us the term, "king's ransom."

Richard I of England, known to history as "Coeur de Lion," was a romantic fellow who much preferred following a quest in full armor to the routine of royal administration. Logically enough, then, he helped organize the Third Crusade and had a lot of fun jousting

Joseph (opposite page) being sold into slavery by his brothers.
(Top left) He interprets Pharaoh's dreams.
(Below) A rare occurrence in kidnappings, the reunion of Joseph and his father.

3

with his foes on the sands of Palestine. On his way to return in triumph to England, he was kidnapped in Austria in 1192 by Duke Leopold. The abduction was illegal under both civil and religious laws, since on the one hand peace existed between England and the Holy Roman Empire and, on the other, no crusader was supposed to be detained by anyone while enroute to or from the Holy Land. Far from punishing his vassal, however, Emperor Henry VI demanded the royal prisoner from the Duke, and lodged him in a castle on the Danube while awaiting the payment of a ransom of 150,000 marks ($15 million). The sum was twice the annual revenue of the British crown and Richard's brother, Prince John, was in no hurry to pay it. Some even suspected that John was paying the Emperor to keep Richard in prison while John conspired to seize the vacant throne.

The merchants of England, newly emerging as a middle class with power, had been able to endure Richard's performance as knight-in-armor, but they feared his brother. John was a greedy operator whom the merchants felt would inevitably try to curtail the power and wealth of his people. Believing thus, it was sensible that they would start a fund to pay the king's ransom. They succeeded in raising the whole amount, and in 1194 Richard came home to wild rejoicing. But, indifferent as always to politics, he did not punish John. So it was that five years later when Richard was killed in a minor battle, John became king.

The anticipated problems arose and soon King John faced revolt. He surrendered and signed the Magna Carta, the document on which the liberties of the English-speaking world are based. In the centuries since, it has proven many times more valuable than a king's ransom.

However, the money paid to ransom Richard fades into insignificance when compared to the

(Opposite page, top) Richard the Lion Hearted and (below) his kidnapper Leopold, Duke of Austria.
(Top) Blondel De Nesle, a 12th-century French troubador who accompanied Richard on the Crusade of 1192. When Richard was imprisoned, Blondel discovered his whereabouts and made himself known to Richard by singing a song they had composed together. This song is the theme of the opera, *Richard, Coeur de Lion*, by Sedaine and Gretry.
(Bottom) Richard's brother, John, who succeeded him on the throne of England, being forced to sign the Magna Carta by his rebellious nobles.

first big kidnapping of the Western world in 1532.

The Spanish were swarming all over Central and South America in search of cities of gold. Many were disappointed, but Francisco Pizarro found wealth beyond his conception in the Inca Empire. With a handful of men Pizarro penetrated deep into what today is Peru. As they had been in Mexico, the Spaniards were welcomed as gods, but Pizarro knew the misconception would not last. How then could a few hundred men seize and keep control of a nation with thousands of experienced warriors? By treachery, of course.

Atahualpa, the Inca ruler, was invited to visit Pizarro's camp in the town of Cajamarca. In the center of the town was a triangular-shaped square surrounded by high walls. The Inca emperor came to the square with only a few hundred warriors as bodyguard. Had he not been too proud to appear afraid in the eyes of his followers, he could have surrounded Pizarro with a hundred thousand men.

In the square, asked to acknowledge the power of Christ and the superiority of the Spanish king, Atahualpa pointed to the sun and stated: "My god still lives."

With that Pizarro dropped his handkerchief. A cannon boomed, and from out of hiding places around the square poured Spanish troops, on horse and on foot. The Inca warriors died bravely in an attempt to protect their king and god; the battle was a massacre. Pizarro intervened at the last minute to save Atahualpa's life. He had a use for it.

A prisoner now, Atahualpa bargained to retain that life. He proposed that his people be allowed to ransom him. He suggested ransom of a great hall filled as high as a man could reach with gold. Pizarro agreed, never believing the price could be met, for the hall in question was twenty-two feet long and seventeen feet wide. Moreover the line drawn in red along the walls was seven feet high.

D. FRAN.^{co} PIZARRO CONQUIS.^{Dor} D.PEF

(Opposite page) An imaginative 18th-century version of Atahualpa's capture. The ambush actually took place inside Cajamarca (rear). (Top) Francisco Pizarro. (Below) Atahualpa, his hostage.

Nevertheless, the idea of allowing the natives to collect and bring in their treasure appealed to the Spaniard. It would save his men a lot of trouble. Two months were allotted to the task. For good measure Pizarro demanded that an adjoining hall be filled not once but twice with silver.

Collection of the treasure took longer than expected and the deadline was extended. Five months after the kidnapping of Atahualpa, the gold was still coming in but the Spaniards were becoming restless. Pizzarro decided to divide the loot. Its value was estimated to be 1,326,539 gold pesos, or, in today's currency, about $170 million.

It is perhaps ironic that Atahualpa still expected to be released. Pizarro knew better. The structure of the empire was built upon complete devotion to the Inca emperor. Remove him, Pizarro thought and, hopefully, the empire would collapse. Now that his financial greed had been satisfied, the exigencies of power had to be considered.

The emperor was accused of plotting against the Spaniards and given a mock trial. The sentence was death by burning. This was doubly cruel for the Incas believed that the soul died if the body was burned. Pizarro was sympathetic. When Atahualpa agreed to become a Christian, his sentence was changed to death by strangulation. And thus died "Juan de Atahualpa" on July 16, 1533. An emperor's ransom had not saved him.

The settlement of the new world, both in North and South America, was greatly expedited by the practice of kidnapping. The first victims were white children from poverty-stricken families and later it was blacks of all ages from Africa. The Lucayans, natives of the Caribbean who settled the Bahama Islands off Florida, were the first to greet Columbus—and they paid dearly for the honor. By 1513, more than 40,000 had been kidnapped by the Spaniards and carried to Cuba to work as slaves on newly developed plantations. The Bahamas were left largely deserted and in subsequent years served as way stations for New England merchants engaged in importing what they euphemistically called "black ivory." Then pirates discovered the Bahamas and after them came the rumrunners and syndicate gamblers. Alas for the Lucayans

CAUTION!!

COLORED PEOPLE

OF BOSTON, ONE & ALL,

You are hereby respectfully CAUTIONED and advised, to avoid conversing with the

Watchmen and Police Officers
of Boston,

For since the recent ORDER OF THE MAYOR & ALDERMEN, they are empowered to act as

KIDNAPPERS
AND

Slave Catchers,

And they have already been actually employed in KIDNAPPING, CATCHING, AND KEEPING SLAVES. Therefore, if you value your LIBERTY, and the *Welfare of the Fugitives* among you, Shun them in every possible manner, as so many *HOUNDS* on the track of the most unfortunate of your race.

Keep a Sharp Look Out for KIDNAPPERS, and have TOP EYE open.

APRIL 24, 1851.

(Opposite page) Arab slave traders in Africa in the 19th century.
(Above) A Boston proclamation in 1851.

—the "boys" named a casino after them.

Kidnapping also has a long history in China and other ports of call in the mysterious East. Before the Communists gained power and outlawed free enterprise, kidnapping flourished. The most lucrative trade was in concubines.

Chinese men believed that several women were necessary to a male's happiness, and those who could afford to do so maintained "stables" almost as large as Solomon's harem. But Western ideas brought monogamy, and conflict. Rich men had to be respectable and so their concubines were forced underground, which offered the kidnapper his opportunity. The men wanted their favorite bedmates back but didn't want wives or associates to know of their old-fashioned taste for concubines. So, rather than tell police and risk exposure, ransoms were regularly paid.

Inevitably, however, the kidnappers ran their good thing into the ground. When a reaction finally set in, captured kidnappers were likely to have their heads cut off in summary justice. But still the practice persisted, until the Communists took power.

However, the modern history of kidnapping as we know it in the Western world can be said to have begun early in April of 1870, when some wealthy English aristocrats visited Greece. Lord and Lady Muncaster were accompanied by Frederick Vyner, a young man of breeding and grace. Such persons were warmly welcomed by the British minister and his staff and every effort was made to keep the tourists amused. A visit to the battlefield of Marathon, some six hours away by horseback was proposed.

On April 11 the expedition started forth. Aware that bandits were plentiful and ruthless in that part of the country, the Greeks provided an armed escort. All went well at first; Marathon was reached and explored. A lunch packed back at the Hotel d'Engleterre was devoured and at about 2 P.M. the party started back to Athens. The escort was suddenly reinforced by a patrol of twelve

仙 逸 孫

Sun Yat-sen (above), kidnapped by
members of his own government and
held prisoner in the Chinese consulate
in London in the 1890's.
(Right) Money used in China from
before World War I up to the
Communist regime.

Sun Yat-sen (center) with his officer corps when he took over the government of China.

(Opposite page) Kidnapping was
prevalent in China for many, many
years. Execution of some members of
a notorious kidnapping gang led by
Lone Cat after they were captured in
a shootout.
(Top) They are executed by being
strangled and (below) shot.
Chiang Kai-shek was kidnapped by a
Chinese warlord, Marshal Chang, in
1936 and held hostage.
(Above) In the happier times of 1893,
Marshal Chang, Mrs. Kung, Mrs. Chang
and General and Mrs. Chiang Kai-shek.

(Above) Lord Muncaster.
(Below) The news clipping of
his kidnap.

DAY, APRIL 25, 1870.

CAPTURED AND MURDERED BY BRIGANDS.

We have been favoured with the following particulars, the substance of which is derived from a letter written by Lord Muncaster :—

" On Saturday, the 9th of April, Lord Muncaster, who, with Lady Muncaster and a friend, Mr. Frederick Vyner, a younger brother of Lady de Grey and Ripon, was travelling in the East, applied, through the British Legation at Athens, for information as to the safety of visiting the plains of Marathon, and if an escort was necessary and could be furnished to enable them to do so.

" The reply was to the effect that the road was safe ; that there were no brigands in Attica, but that an escort would be provided. Accordingly, on Monday, the 11th of April, at 6 30 a.m., the party, consisting of Lord and Lady Muncaster, Mr. Frederick Vyner, Mr. Herbert, one of the Secretaries to Her Majesty's Legation, Count de Boyl, Secretary to the Italian Legation, and Mr. and Mrs. Lloyd, with their young child, five years of age, left Athens in two carriages under the escort of four mounted gendarmes for Marathon, accompanied by a Suliote named Alexandros, the most experienced and intelligent dragoman in Greece.

" On traversing the plain   und a small detachment of six infantry   afterwards a

policemen—on foot. This slowed the march considerably. Gradually the footmen fell behind. After more than two hours the party had become somewhat disorganized, and then brigands struck. Some thirty armed men leaped out of the bushes, shot the guards nearest to the English visitors, and dragged their victims into the woods.

Leader of the kidnappers was Takos Arvenitakis, a colorful outlaw who had learned to fight while serving with the Greek army against the Turks and to steal while serving in several political posts. Despite his status as a brigand, he was sometimes employed unofficially by the government in missions not unlike those performed by a more modern group known as the "Plumbers."

However, the kidnapping of the titled English visitors definitely did not have government approval, unofficial or otherwise, and Takos knew there would be heavy pressure. Nevertheless he drafted a letter demanding ransom in the amount of a million drachmas, or approximately $500,000 in today's currency. Lady Muncaster was released to carry the letter. Takos gave her two captured soldiers to serve as guard and, as a gesture of admiration, a silver pendant of the virgin he habitually wore around his own neck. Lord Muncaster was not amused.

Greek officials sent an emissary to bargain with Takos and eventually the size of the ransom was reduced somewhat. The Ionian Bank of Athens, on assurances from England, advanced the money and hopes were high for the release of the prisoners. But then Takos demanded a pardon. This, the Greek government, a rather shaky institution, did not dare do. So the government indicated that Takos wouldn't be stopped if he and his men decided to cross the border into Turkey after collecting the money.

Things might have worked out on that basis. In fact, a British destroyer, the *Cockatrice,* was steaming full speed from Malta to Athens with instructions to carry Takos and his crew to any port in the Mediterranean world they cared to visit. But politics interfered. Men believed to represent the not-so-loyal opposition to the Greek government sent a delegation to Takos and convinced him he was being cheated. In addition to Lady Muncaster, he had also released her husband as a gesture of good faith, which he was told was a mistake. Takos was told that Lord Muncaster was a cousin of Queen Victoria, although this was a lie. Moreover, why accept safe conduct into Turkey when the Turks would simply seize him and his loot?

Convinced he had been tricked, Takos repudiated the terms agreed upon. The Greek government, apparently aware of the intrigue, decided on a show of military force to convince Takos that his escape depended upon cooperation. This was a mistake, since outlaw tradition had long held that any military action against Greek bandits must be answered by the immediate execution of prisoners. Vyner and two of his friends were immediately disembowelled and allowed to bleed to death.

While the prisoners were being tortured, the government troops closed in. Six bandits were killed and a number captured. The bodies were recovered, but Takos escaped and disappeared.

In England, Queen Victoria was furious. The press and public demanded that Greece be taught a lesson. Only Prime Minister Gladstone kept cool—he saw no point in punishing a nation for the crimes of a few outlaws. Reportedly, Victoria became so angry she refused to speak to the Prime Minister for a full year. An inquiry in Greece disclosed that the Minister of War, who had mismanaged the affair from the start, was a large landowner in the area where the brigands operated and had, in fact, cooperated with them. He was forced to resign.

The Greek tragedy was shortly thereafter followed by a uniquely American tragedy—the first of many.

The "Gold Conspiracy" in 1870 tarnished the image of President U.S. Grant and created widespread cynicism. The exposure of the

(Above) Queen Victoria.
(Below) Her Prime Minister, Gladstone.

Tweed Ring in New York City in 1871 added to the growing distrust of politicians and businessmen. And in 1872 the *Credit Mobilier* scandal threatened to break open and defeat Grant's bid for re-election. Jay Cooke, one of the nation's foremost "robber barons," was able to delay the scandal until 1873, but then the dam broke. Congressional hearings disclosed that *Credit Mobilier,* the company that built the first transcontinental railroad, was steeped in fraud. More than $50 million had been stolen, and the list of those implicated included high government officials as well as businessmen at home and abroad.

Cooke's financial empire was threatened but he assured his brother of his faith that God "will not desert us." He still felt confident on September 17, 1873, when he entertained President Grant at "Ogontz," the Philadelphia palace Cooke called home. But the next day his bank went broke. As one writer put it:

> The largest and most pious bank in the Western world had fallen with the effect of a thunderclap. Soon allied brokers and national banks and 5,000 commercial houses followed it into the abyss of bankruptcy.

The panic was on, and after it came a grim economic recession. The winter of 1873–74 found tens of thousands of people near starvation. Millions were unemployed. Riots were frequent, and children cried for bread.

As the months passed things got worse instead of better, and on July 1, 1874, four-year-old Charlie Ross was kidnapped from his home in the Germantown part of Philadelphia.

It was a hot day and Charlie was playing under the shade of old trees with his brother, Walter, when a shabby buggy rattled up Washington Lane. The boys remembered it from the previous week when two nice men in it had given them candy and offered them a ride. The same two men were in the buggy that day and again they stopped and again they made a proposition. Instead of candy, some firecrackers were the bait. With the glorious Fourth only three days away, the bait was irresistible. The boys climbed in.

After a long ride the carriage stopped. Walter, two years older than Charlie, was given a quarter and told to go into the store across the street and buy whatever he pleased. Walter obeyed, and took his time about deciding. Some fifteen minutes later, when he returned to the street with his investment, the carriage was gone. There was no sign of his brother or the nice strangers. Walter began to cry.

A passerby took pity. Walter disclosed the name of his father, Christian K. Ross, a

16

prosperous storekeeper. By 8 P.M. the boy was back home. But where was Charlie? Police were called, but neither the father nor the cops could believe that foul play was involved. It seemed unkind, somehow, to suggest it. Obviously, they concluded, Charlie had been sent on a similar shopping spree and had somehow got lost.

Mrs. Ross might have had other ideas, but she was vacationing at Atlantic City. The father placed an advertisement about a little boy lost in the daily newspaper next day, being careful not to mention names for fear someone might needlessly alarm Mrs. Ross.

Two days later a letter arrived, postmarked Philadelphia. The handwritten message:

Mr. Ross:

Be not uneasy you son Charlie be all writ we is got him and no powers on earth can deliver out of our hand. you will have to pay us befor you git him from us, and pay us a big cent to if you regard his lif puts no one in search for him you mony can fech him out alive an no other existin powers. you here from us in a few days.

(Opposite page, left) President Grant and (right) Jay Cooke.
(Above) Some editorial cartoons of the day dealing with Boss Tweed's corruption of New York City government.

Mrs. Ross had returned by now and any inclination the father might have had to resist the demands disappeared quickly at the sight of her stricken face. Three days later the second letter came. Misspelled and poorly punctuated, it, nevertheless, communicated the ransom demand: $20,000. The note warned grimly:

if you love money more than child yu be its murderer not us . . . if we get yu money yu get him live if no money you get him ded

Ross was told to run an ad in the paper when he had the money ready. Meanwhile, the story broke in the newspapers and quickly became a national sensation. The police, completely bewildered, made a house-to-house search of the city, and achieved nothing. Hysteria developed. Women whose children looked something like the missing Charlie brought their tykes to Ross and pleaded for a signed certificate saying the child wasn't Charlie. Other mothers were convinced their child would be the next victim. In an age of public cynicism such as then existed, there seemed no security anywhere.

Ross put the message in the papers: the money was ready. But the kidnappers were suspicious, and the exchange of messages continued. Four weeks passed. By then it had become apparent that the kidnappers were intelligent and cautious. Their notes were obviously contrived to appear illiterate. Sometimes a simple word was misspelled in one note and spelled correctly in another.

Meanwhile, with hysteria mounting, a public meeting was held, at which the mayor of Philadelphia presided. A reward of $20,000 for the kidnappers was posted.

The next letter was postmarked in New York City. It ordered Ross to take a midnight train to New York, change there for Albany and to stand on the rear platform all night. When, somewhere along the way, he saw a white flag waved from the ground he was to toss a bag containing the ransom to the side. If all was well with the money, and if Ross and the train continued to Albany without stopping, the child would be released.

On the advice of police, Ross made the trip

Mr. Ros— July 3
you Don be not uneasy
ot him al sirit we is
in earth and no powers
i of our hand— you
for you git him from
is— an pay us a big
the cops hunting for him
you is only defeeting
you own end—

(Opposite page, top) Little Charlie Ross,
the stolen child, and (below) his
brother who was abducted with him
but escaped.
(Top) Part of the ransom note and
(left) a sketch of the abduction.

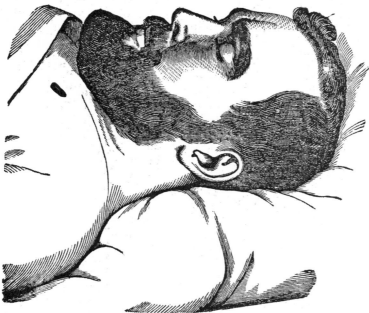

(Top) The burglars Mosher and Douglas were shot while robbing Judge Van Brunt's house, in Brooklyn.
(Below), Douglas, the burglar, after he was shot.
(Opposite page, top) Bill Mosher, the burglar.
(Opposite page, below) Part of a Pinkerton reward poster. The reward had been gradually increased from $5,000 to $20,000 as time passed and the child was not found.

$20,000 REWARD

~~has~~ been offered for the recovery of CHARLIE BREWSTER ROSS,
~~for~~ the arrest and conviction of his abductors. He was
~~stolen~~ from his parents in Germantown, Pa., on July 1st, 1874,
~~by~~ two unknown men.

DESCRIPTION OF THE CHILD.

but the bag he carried contained only a letter demanding proof that Charlie was still alive. The kidnappers were cautious too—no flag waved in the night and the letter was not delivered. Months passed. It was November before another appointment was made to deliver the cash—this time in a New York hotel. But no one appeared. Ross hired private detectives, offered a $5,000 reward, and all to no avail.

On December 14 two men attempted to rob a judge's home in Brooklyn. A burglar alarm sounded and when the men emerged they were gunned down. As one of them lay dying he muttered:

"My name is Joseph Douglas. That man there is Mosher. Mosher and I stole Charlie Ross. Mosher will tell you about it."

But Mosher was dead.

Douglas, still alive, was asked where the boy was hidden.

"He'll be returned in five days," said the bullet-riddled burglar. "Chief Walling knows all about us."

Walling was the police chief of New York.

Confirmation that Mosher and Douglas were indeed the kidnappers came from Walter Ross, brother of the missing boy. At the morgue in New York, he identified the dead men as the two who had taken him to buy fireworks.

The five days passed and there was still silence. Charlie Ross remained missing. The police chief claimed that he had indeed known about Mosher and Douglas, and had been trying to develop one of their friends, an ex-cop, as an informer in an effort to find the boy. Somehow, it sounded rather fishy.

Mrs. Mosher was questioned and admitted she had known about the kidnapping but did not know where Charlie was being kept. She was sure, however, that her husband had not harmed him.

Why had Mosher done it? "Poverty," said Mrs. Mosher. With four children to feed and no work to be had, men became desperate.

The months became years and nothing was heard from Charlie Ross. There were plenty of pretenders, however; the distraught father later reported that he had personally investigated 273 children said to be his son. As late as 1927, a claim was made by a middle-aged man. But from the real victim there was only silence—the silence of the grave, perhaps.

Meanwhile, the continuing scandals were much investigated and it was written that the evidence "led into the parlor of the President."

Sound familiar?

A quarter-century passed without a kidnapping of note. People still talked of the Ross case as the most sensational crime. Then in 1900 came the kidnapping of Eddie Cudahy.

Edward A. Cudahy, Sr., was perhaps the richest man in Omaha, Nebraska; his meat-packing business was one of the giants of the industry. The heir apparent was fifteen-year-old Eddie, a popular and apparently well-respected boy.

On the evening of December 18, the father asked his son to deliver a package of old magazines to a doctor's office, presumably to decorate the doctor's waiting room. That a doctor should accept secondhand magazines from the town's richest man tells something of the social and economic conditions then prevailing.

Eddie complied, dropping off the magazines about 7 P.M. and starting home immediately. But he was suddenly confronted by two men with drawn pistols, who announced they were detectives. They accused young Cudahy of being a robber named McGee.

Eddie denied it, but the men pushed him into a buggy and started off to—they said—police headquarters. Confident the matter would soon be straightened out, the youth relaxed. But suddenly the buggy stopped on a dark, deserted street, and the "detectives" tied Eddie's arms, put a gag in his mouth and a bandage over his eyes. Then the buggy ride resumed. After about an hour they reached an old house, inside which Eddie was then

The Cudahy mansion and the kidnapped boy. (Opposite page) News clippings of the day.

DISPATCH MARKET REPORT.

ST. LOUIS

St. Louis Millionaires
Tell St. Louis Young Men How to Get
Rich, in the
SUNDAY POST-DISPATCH.....

ST. LOUIS

THE ONLY ST. LOUIS EVEN

VOL. 53, NO. 122.   FRIDAY EVENING

MOVED BY HIS WIFE'S AGONY

Why Cudahy Yielded to the Kidnappers' Terms.

FEARED TO THWART THEM

POLICE DEVISING PLANS TO RUN DOWN THE CRIMINALS.

One Theory Is That the Brigands Were Headed by Pat Crowe, Burglar and Train Robber, Well Known to the St. Louis Police.

SOME FAMOUS KIDNAPPINGS

The abduction of Charlie Ross is one of the most famous cases of the kind on record. He was a boy of 5 playing in the street in front of his father's home at Germantown, Pa., when he was carried off by two men July 1, 1874. A ransom of $20,000 was demanded for the boy, and his father's friends wanted to pay it, but the police held them back, hoping to find him. They never did. The father spent his fortune and became insane in the search, which lasted 18 years. It is supposed Charlie and his captors were such

EDWARD A. CUDAHY.
The Omaha Millionaire Who Paid Kidnappers $25,000 for the return of His 15-Year-Old Boy.

F
p

ST
L

At
Hick
G
fre

161,   4   VOL. 53, NO. 12   IR FUND BY
                                    NEW YEAR'S DAY

MILLIONAIRE E. A. CUDAHY
FOR RETURN OF HIS SON
PAYS KIDNAPPERS $25,000

Carried the Money, All in Gold, to a Point Five Miles From Omaha, and at Midnight Deposited It Where Abductors Had Placed a Lantern.

In a Short Time the Missing Boy Was Returned to His Home.

THE LAD IS 15 YEARS OLD

GAGG   CHAINED AND GUARD

INCIDENTS OF
THE ABDUCTION.

The kidnapped boy is the son of Edward Cudahy, millionaire, of Omaha, and member of the well-known packing firm of Cudahy Bros.

The boy, who is 15 years old, was stolen Tuesday evening, while on the streets of Omaha.

Wednesday the father received two letters demanding $25,000 for the son's return.

handcuffed to a chair and given food. His captors drank a lot of liquor.

Meanwhile, back at the mansion at 518 South 37th Street, the parents began first to wonder at Eddie's absence and then to worry. Cudahy telephoned the doctor and learned that Eddie had left two hours before. A man of decision, Cudahy wasted no time. He called the police and got the respectful reaction a man in his position expected. Not content, he sent word to his employees that Eddie was either lost or kidnapped. A search began immediately. The entire town was checked before morning. By daylight it was clear that Eddie wasn't lost. Cudahy immediately offered a reward and promised to ask no questions if his son was returned. For good measure, however, he sent for twenty Pinkerton detectives from Chicago.

It was still only 9 A.M. when a man on horseback rode at a gallop past the Cudahy home and tossed an envelope to the lawn. It contained a ransom demand which was quickly proved a hoax. A little later in the day the coachman found a stick with a red cloth attached stuck in the lawn. Tied to the stick was a letter. Addressed to Cudahy, it said in part:

We have kidnapped your child and demand twenty-five thousand dollars for his safe return. If you give us the money, the child will be returned as safe as when you last saw him; but if you refuse, we will put acid in his eyes and blind him . . .

Get the money all in gold—five, ten, and twenty dollar pieces—put it in a grip in a white wheat sack, get in your buggy alone on the night of December 19, at seven o'clock P.M., and drive south from your house to Center Street and drive back to Ruser's Park and follow the paved road toward Fremont.

When you come to a lantern that is lighted by the side of the road, place your money by the lantern and immediately turn your horse around and return home. You will know our lantern, for it will have two ribbons, black and white, tied on the handle. You must place a red lantern on your buggy where it can be plainly seen, so we will know you a mile away . . .

(Opposite page, below) Pat Crowe, the kidnapper, and (above) some Boer commandos, the type of soldier Crowe fought with in the war.

If you remember, some twenty years ago Charley Ross was kidnapped in New York City, and twenty thousand dollars ransom asked. Old man Ross was willing to give up the money, but Byrnes, the great detective, with others, persuaded the old man not to give up the money, assuring him the thieves would be captured. Ross died of a broken heart, sorry that he allowed the detectives to dictate to him . . .

Mr. Cudahy, you are up against it, there is only one way out. Give up the coin. Money we want, and money we will get. If you don't give it up, the next man will, for he will see we mean business, and you can lead your boy around blind for the rest of your days and all you will have is the damn copper's sympathy.

The police, as usual, urged Cudahy not to pay, but Mrs. Cudahy insisted that her husband pay the ransom. "What's twenty-five thousand dollars compared to my boy?" she reportedly asked.

The banks had closed by the time the father made up his mind, but that was no problem. The First National Bank was happy to cooperate, and on Cudahy's order made up five bags of gold containing the ransom. The combined weight of the bags was more than one hundred pounds. Fixing the red lantern to the buggy, Cudahy loaded up the gold and departed on his desperate mission.

The night was dark and the air was cold. Cudahy carried a pistol as much to guard against possible hijackers as perhaps to use in rescuing Eddie. And soon, up ahead, he saw a lantern tied to a tree limb by black and white ribbons. There was no sound, no sign of life. He put the wheat sack containing the five bags of gold beside the tree. Still there was only silence. Slowly, he got back into the buggy, turned it around, and headed home. It was a ten-mile ride.

The mother was of course disappointed when her husband returned without her son, and the police were sure the kidnappers would demand a second ransom payment. As they talked, a sound was heard. Mrs. Cudahy was

first to recognize it. Eddie was coming up the
walk. She rushed out to meet him and
glimpsed two men running down the street.
But it was only a glimpse, and she embraced
her grinning son.

Once the safety of the boy was assured, the
police apparently did a creditable job of
investigation. Aided by a few scanty clues
supplied by Eddie, they located the house in
which he had been held within the city limits.
It developed that one farmer had sold the
occupants of that house a buggy and another
had sold them a horse. Adding up the several
descriptions and comparing them to known
criminals of the area, the police decided that
the mastermind was a romantic fellow named
Pat Crowe.

It made sense. Crowe had been fired by
Cudahy's people ten years before and had
turned to train robbing as a substitute for meat
packing. Moreover, he was known to be
fearless and a crack shot. Giving more weight
to the idea of Crowe's involvement was the
fact that he had been seen in Omaha the day
before the kidnapping, but could not now be
located. An alarm went out and soon Crowe
was being "spotted" from Mexico City to
Singapore. Actually, he was in Africa. As he
later admitted, he left Omaha by horseback
within minutes of collecting the ransom.
Catching a train at a way station, he had gone
on to Chicago and then to New York, where
he boarded a ship for South Africa. The gold
went with him. The Boer War was under way,
and so Crowe signed up with the underdog
Boers in their battle against the British. He
was wounded twice, decorated for bravery, and
became something of a hero.

Having achieved the "perfect crime," so to
speak, Crowe's criminal ambitions were
satisfied and somewhere along the way he
decided to go straight. This impulse to honesty
caused him to send money to an Omaha
attorney in 1905 to repay the old debt. It was
the first real clue as to his whereabouts.

Shortly thereafter, Crowe returned to New

(Above) President McKinley, of whom
Teddy Roosevelt said, "He has a
spine like an eclair."
(Right) Roosevelt on the campaign trail.

York. Rewards for his capture totaled $55,000, but, unabashed, he walked into the City Room of a New York newspaper and gave an interview. Having put his side of the story forward, he offered to surrender if the rewards were withdrawn. His terms were finally accepted and Crowe gave himself up. As if trying to prove that his decision to turn honest was sincere, he freely admitted his part in the kidnapping.

But Crowe in so doing had not lost his mind. While he had been fighting in Africa, much had happened in the United States. Of these, the most important was the death of President William McKinley on September 14, 1901, the victim of an assassin's bullet. While well beloved, McKinley had done little to interfere with the robber barons of his day. His successor, "that damned cowboy," Theodore Roosevelt, said McKinley had a "backbone of chocolate eclair." Now Roosevelt was President and his first objective was to bust the trusts. Among the first to feel his wrath was the meat-packing industry in which Cudahy was so prominent. Public opinion was being swayed, meanwhile, by the "Muckrakers." It was no coincidence that Crowe's decision to

surrender in 1906 came shortly after the publication of Upton Sinclair's novel about the meat industry, *The Jungle*. The book, Sinclair said later, was aimed at America's heart but hit its stomach instead. Be that as it may, it contributed to the unique situation in which Cudahy seemed a black villain and Crowe a Robin Hood.

The trial began. Despite Crowe's admissions, he was acquitted. His accomplice was also acquitted. The verdict was greeted with cheers from a crowed courtroom. Journalists discovered that the popular theory of the affair was now that Cudahy had arranged the whole thing just to get free advertising for his beef.

Crowe went on to write a book about his exploits and became a lecturer. His theme: "The big fortunes that have been made in this country have been mostly made by men who have broken the criminal law in building them up—the same law that has been used against me."

In that era of cynicism about big business, this thesis seemed viable. Years later, when Eddie became head of his father's business, he received a message: "Congratulations, Eddie, from your old kidnapper."

Social commentary of the times: Teddy Roosevelt raking through the meat scandal.

2. ALL FOR "A LITTLE KNOWLEDGE"

Organized crime is not born full grown with machine guns blazing. It develops slowly from a sick society—a society blighted by economic conditions and political corruption.

Such a society had long existed in the steel towns of eastern Ohio. Youngstown was perhaps the center of the area which extended into nearby Pennsylvania to the east and into West Virginia to the southeast.

In the 1930's the Cleveland Syndicate turned from rum-running across Lake Erie to illegal gambling. Soon it had outposts in several states and in time would expand to Miami, Las Vegas, and Havana. The Youngstown area became part of its political domain, and such plush gambling joints at the Jungle Inn came under its control. However, gambling in the area was pretty small stuff—*barbut,* a multiple dice game, and the numbers racket. These games were left largely to the local operators, many of whom belonged to that disorganized, vendetta-ridden society known as the Mafia.

It was not until the 1950's, after the Cleveland "boys" turned respectable in Nevada, that the nation as a whole became aware of conditions in and around Youngstown. A typical Mafia struggle for control of *barbut* broke into open warfare and men were shot or blasted with bombs in incredible numbers. In time, the killings ceased as a reform movement attempted to civilize the area and teach respect for law and order. Little changed, however, as far as the rackets were concerned.

The kidnapping of Willie Whitla in 1909 provides some insight into conditions that later were to make Youngstown synonymous with murder.

Actually, Willie lived in Sharon, Pennsylvania, just across the line from Ohio and twenty-five miles east of Warren. His father, James P. Whitla, was a leading attorney and, more important, nephew of steel overlord Frank M. Buhl. Buhl was to Sharon what Cudahy had been to Omaha, and so young Willie was a priviledged character even as a relative of the great man.

One cold March day in 1909 Willie was, as usual, in school. Outside, a buggy drove up. In it was a short, dark fellow who told the janitor

he was there at Mr. Whitla's direction to bring
Willie to his father's office. The janitor
conveyed the message to Willie's teacher who
hastened to obey. She helped the eight-year-old
put on his coat and escorted him outside to
the buggy. The driver didn't impress her very
much and she remarked to the janitor: "I hope
that man doesn't kidnap Willie."

Willie was happy at first to have escaped his
geography class, but as the buggy crossed the
river and headed down the road toward Ohio,
he began to wonder. The man gave him cheese
sandwiches to quiet him, but Willie kept
asking when they would see papa.

Back home, Mrs. Whitla wondered why
Willie didn't come home as usual for lunch,
but his absence didn't worry her. Late that
afternoon, however, she became frantic. The
postman brought a letter addressed to her in
Willie's childish scrawl, but inside was a letter
from a kidnapper. It said:

*We have your boy, and no harm will come to him
if you comply with our instructions. If you give this
letter to the newspapers or divulge any of its contents,
you will never see your boy again. We demand ten
thousand dollars in twenty dollar, ten dollar, and five
dollar bills. If you attempt to mark the money, or
place counterfeit money, you will be sorry. Dead men
tell no tales. Neither do dead boys. You may answer
at the following addresses: Cleveland Press,
Youngstown Vindicator, Indianapolis News, and
Pittsburgh Dispatch in the personal columns. Answer
"A.A. will do as you requested, J.P.W."*

Mrs. Whitla put in a long-distance call to
her husband, who was out of town. She
notified a friend. The friend called the police.
Within two hours the story had spread across
the eastern half of the country and the alert
was on in several states. A boy who knew
Willie reported seeing him get out of a buggy
on the road to Warren and mail a letter. In
Warren a horse and buggy was found with
Willie's hat upon the seat. The rig had been
rented earlier that day in Sharon.

Meanwhile, Willie's father hurried home and

The sink in Willie's prison where he
was hidden whenever capture was near.
(Right) News clipping of the crime.

ST. LOUIS POST-DISPATCH

Only Evening Paper in St. Louis with both Associated Press and United Press Servi

NO. 212.   ST. LOUIS, SATURDAY EVENING, MARCH 20, 1909.   PRIC

PHOTOGRAPHS OF THE STOLEN BOY AND HIS FATHER, AND MAP OF TERRITORY BEING SEARCHED FOR KIDNAPERS

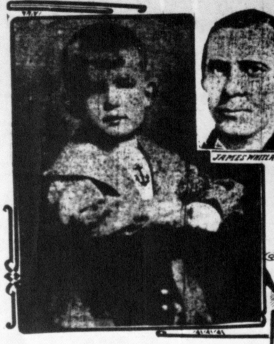

JAMES WHITLA

WILLIE WHITLA

CLEVELAND   SHARON   YOUNGSTOWN   PENN.   PITTSBURG   INDIANAPOLIS   INDIANA   OHIO

CLEVELAND BOY IS NOT KIDNAPED BILLY WHITLA

Millionaire Uncle Finds Child Is Not Nephew, and Says He Will Open Negotiations to Pay $10,000 Ransom.

Special to the Post-Dispatch.
CLEVELAND, 0., March 20.—That
Kidnaped Billy Whitla is not in Cleveland and has not been here is the con-
clusion which both the police and
the boy's millionaire
today when
Euclid Ho-
and his

the father who was also a friend of
J. P. Whitla, spent nearly every cent
he had in trying to get a trace of his
child. A year later a peddler discovered the kidnaped child in a home at
Punxsutawney, Pa. It had been
left by a man a

MRS. LAMBERT IS WARNED BY "JOE" AGAINST DRINK

"Shun Cl

The Whitla family reunited. (Left to right) Willie, Mrs. Whitla, Selina
Whitla and father, James.

conferred with his uncle. Both men were
accustomed to threats. Only a month earlier
Buhl, the steel magnate, had received a Black
Hand extortion letter demanding $5,000. A
writer of the period noted: "Mr. Buhl,
however, was hardened to the tactics of this
lawless region, filled with low-grade Italians,
Slovaks, etc., and ignored it as he had many
others before." But Willie was already missing.
Buhl decided to offer a $10,000, reward for
Willie's safe return and a $20,000 reward for
each and every one of the kidnappers—dead or
alive.

Whitla was a lawyer, of course, and familiar
with the outcome of the Charlie Ross and
the Cudahy cases. In the latter, he knew,
the police had been ignored, the ransom
paid, and the victim recovered, but it had
not been so in the Ross episode. So, while his
uncle took a hard line for the benefit of
the press and police, Whitla quietly
inserted the specified message in the
newspapers.

Assurance that Willie was still alive came in

a personal note from the boy. It read:

*Two bad men have me They will kill me if you
don't send $10,000. Willie.*

Two days after Whitla's ad appeared, a
letter arrived from the kidnappers with
instructions for paying the ransom. Whitla was
directed to go to the park in an isolated
section of the nearby city of Ashtabula, Ohio.
There he was to locate a certain cannon
mounted on a rock and behind it he was to
place the money. If all went well he could then
return to the local hotel where his son would
soon appear.

Whitla obeyed. He told the police he was
going to Cleveland on a business trip. He
doubled back to Ashtabula, however, and
followed all instructions to the letter. Then he
went to the hotel lobby to wait.

Instead of his son, police appeared.
Somehow a second letter from the kidnappers
had been left at the Ashtabula hotel and had
been opened by mistake. The police had been

32

The Hollenden Hotel, Cleveland, Ohio.

notified. They swarmed into the hotel at 3 A.M. to tell the angry Whitla that they had searched Flatiron Park without result. He instantly demanded they cease their efforts, but the police could not be deterred from what they considered their duty. They spent the balance of the night searching boarding houses and back alleys. Not too surprisingly, Willie was not found. And when Whitla returned next morning to the cannon in the park, he found the ransom there untouched. His feelings did not improve when he arrived home in Sharon by train, where a brass band and a delegation of townspeople were waiting to greet Willie. Somehow, word had spread that Whitla had rescued his son, and cheering citizens had gathered at the station. As usual, Willie was being reported all over the country, and scores of suspects were being arrested on general principles. It all added up to frustration for Whitla.

But the kidnappers were persistent. Soon another letter came. The mistake at Ashtabula was acknowledged and Whitla was given new instructions. This time he was to go to Cleveland. At a certain drugstore a letter addressed to William Williams would be waiting. It would contain additional information.

Greatly relieved but more determined to keep the police out of it, he slipped off to Cleveland undetected. The letter at the drugstore sent him to a candy store on East 43rd Street. There he gave the ransom to a woman, as instructed. She gave him in return a note from the kidnappers telling him to go to the Hollenden Hotel and engage a room, that the boy would be returned within three hours.

The Hollenden, ironically, was later to become the headquarters of the Cleveland Syndicate, where bosses operated offices, maintained suites of rooms, and acted in general as if they owned the place. Rivals were later murdered in the hotel and in the alleys outside. And a nest of gambling joints and cheap nightclubs sprang up in the area convenient to the hotel. Nevertheless, it retained its reputation as a plush place to stay —and why not? The syndicate boys could afford the best during the wide-open days in which they controlled Cleveland.

Whitla tried to obey but his tension was too great for the confines of a room. He went down to the lobby and began to march back and forth across the marble tile. A Cleveland reporter noticed him, guessed what was happening, and remained inconspicuous. Two hours passed. Whitla, at last, sank into a deep chair. He was tired, very tired.

Outside the hotel a streetcar stopped. A boy wearing dark goggles and a yellow cap got off, quiet and scared. Two other boys on the streetcar followed him off. Somehow, they suspected that this was the famous Willie—the boy the entire country was seeking. They told their suspicions to a policeman who accompanied them—and the mystery boy— into the hotel.

The clerk at the desk pulled off the goggles and the cap. "Aren't you Willie Whitla?" he asked.

The little boy smiled. "Where is my daddy?" he replied.

The elder Whitla awoke from his self-induced stupor at that point and rushed across the lobby to grasp his son. Everyone cheered—everyone but the reporter who rushed to the telephone to tell his city editor the news.

The band again was waiting next day when the Whitla's returned to Sharon. Joy, as one observer put it, was unrestrained. There was double reason to rejoice—for the kidnappers had been captured the same night.

Shortly after Willie had been reunited with his father, a man and woman appeared in a Cleveland bar and insisted on treating the house. They flashed brand new five dollar bills as if they had an endless supply. The bartender, one Pat O'Reilly, checked the bills and noticed they bore consecutive serial numbers. That was evidence enough for him.

(Opposite page) Willie Whitla greeting his friends and the townspeople of Sharon after his return.
(Left) James H. Bogle, Willie's kidnapper.

He supplied the happy couple with a few "on the house" and when at last they staggered out into the dawn he called the police. The couple was quickly intercepted. The woman, when searched at the station, was found to have $9,790 concealed in her clothes. In drunken pride she announced: "I planned the whole thing."

She proved to be Helen McDermott Bogle, a "loose woman," the newspapers said, who had been drifting around the steel towns of the area for some years. Alas, the newspapers added, she came of good parents and had spent "fifteen years in a convent." Perhaps that is why she had finally married—married a "drifter" named James H. Bogle. They had planned to use the money to buy a little house and settle down, but the release from tension had been too much to bear without a few drinks in celebration.

Willie grew up to be an attorney like his father. When, many years later, another child was stolen and the world waited with the parents in terrified suspense, Willie had a word of reassurance. Based on what had happened to him, he said, he was sure the baby would be returned safely. The Bogles were, after all, pretty nice people. At least they had treated him well enough.

If the Bogles were "nice people" considering their station in life, then Richard Loeb and Nathan F. Leopold, Jr., should have been princes of the blood.

That's what many people considered them to be, as a matter of fact, for both young men were sons of very wealthy parents who had, literally, given them every material thing they had ever wanted.

Born in 1906, three years before Willie was kidnapped, Leopold was something of a mess physically. He was small, round, and inclined to sexual perversity. Although his thyroid gland was undersized, he was something of a genius. He spoke nine languages and was a skilled botanist and ornithologist, but his mother had died when he was young and he was said to have grown up in a loveless house.

Richard Loeb, son of a vice president of

The great crowd welcoming Willie
back to Sharon.
(Right) A news clipping of the event.

RANSOMED BOY IN HIS MOTHER'S ARMS; HOLIDAY IN SHARON

Willie Whitla Home Again—Worth Ten Times $10,000, Says Father to Crowd.

HUNT FOR KIDNAPERS IS ON; PARENTS INDIFFERENT

Police Are Watching Railroad Stations and Lake and Seaports; Bills Paid by Father Were All Marked.

SHARON, Pa., March 23.—Willie Whitla, the ransomed boy, after an experience of five days with kidnapers, was returned to his mother's arms soon after noon today.

The reunion took place around the family hearthstone in the Whitla home, and no prying eyes were permitted to witness the greeting of mother and son, only the immediate relatives of the family being present at the lad's joyful home-coming.

The task now of capturing the abductors is occupying the attention of the detectives. Every bill which went to make up the $10,000 ransom package is known to the officers by number and it is thought possible the kidnapers will be traced in this manner.

The search is now being conducted rigidly since the boy has been recovered and the numbers of the currency were sent to the authorities all over the country. It is reported this afternoon that developments in the case are expected soon at Cleveland and Akron, O., and Indianapolis. What they are is not known except to the detectives, but Mr. Perkins, of Pittsburg is confident that important disclosures at these points will come.

Accorded an ovation by the populace of Sharon that could not have been heartier, the little fellow and his father arrived here at 12:05, after an absence of 125 hours. Fully 5000 persons extended the lad a demonstrative greeting. Pushing their way through the dense crowd surrounding the railroad station, Mr. Whitla, Willie, his uncle and a detective, entered a cab and quickly were driven home.

Cheering and singing, the great gathering of enthusiastic neighbors and citizens followed the cab through the streets. Business practically was at a standstill, public schools were dismissed

By 1:30 o'clock the crowd began to disperse.

From the time the boy left Cleveland this morning until his arrival here this afternoon the trip resembled the triumphal journey of some great personage. At most of the railroad stations crowds gathered to see the boy.

Boy Cheered as He Departed.

CLEVELAND, O., March 23.—Willie Whitla, the kidnaped boy, and James P. Whitla, the rejoicing father, left Cleveland today for Sharon, Pa.

Hundreds clogged the corridors of the Hollenden Hotel, in anticipation of catching a glimpse of the lad whose whereabouts had become a puzzle to the detectives of the land.

"Gee, papa," said the youngster as he was being helped into a taxicab, "I hope mamma is on the front porch waiting for us."

"She will be there," was the simple answer from the father, as he clasped his boy's hand.

The speed of a Cleveland taxicab did not deter hundreds from following to the Erie station, where the Whitlas boarded a train. The father appeared to be the happiest man in Ohio, and Willie professed to believe that a "real choo choo was more better than one of them street engines."

Friedrich Nietzsche.

Sears, Roebuck and Company, was a year younger than Leopold but, physically, he was everything his friend was not. Tall and handsome, he could be charming upon demand. Occasionally he did stutter, and he sometimes blacked out momentarily, but he concealed his defects well. He was also a homosexual. Crime intrigued him and for a time he flirted with the idea of becoming a private detective.

Upon meeting at a party, the boys were immediately attracted to each other. In a word, they fell in love. Soon they developed a relationship that was closer than many between men and women. Their love affair was rocky, however, the immense egos of each of the boys sometimes getting in the way. But they had their fun—committing petty crimes, cheating at cards, "trashing" the homes of their rich friends—but after a while it got rather boring.

Consider the times. President Warren G. Harding died on August 2, 1923, and within weeks the scandal that soon was to be famous as Teapot Dome was making headlines. But cynicism enough existed already. It was the time of F. Scott Fitzgerald and his "Lost Generation." Supposedly all the wars had been fought, all the challenges met. Away with abstraction—the only reality was Republican Prosperity and the supply of bootleg booze. Women were suddenly free to do as they damned well pleased, and many of them did. A British writer looked back some years ago and described the social pattern, "both in the States and in Britain," as "a simple one." Sophisticated but simple. It was based on an absolute and undisputed materialism. "I have a Cadillac. You have not. I am one up on you. My father has a private swimming pool. Yours has not. My father is better than your father. I have a husband and a desirable lover. You only have a husband. How dowdy can you get?"

Late in 1923 the youths began to plan the perfect crime. While the idea came from Loeb, it appealed to Leopold, who was an avid

Nathan Leopold (left) and Richard Loeb
(right) with States Attorney
Robert E. Crone.
(Below) The ransom note.

ar Sir:

As you no doubt know by this time
your son has been kidnapped. Allow us to
assure you that he is at present well and
safe. You need fear no physical harm
provided you live up carefully to the following instructions, and such others as
you will receive by future communication.
Should you however, disobey any of instructions even slightly, his death will
be the penalty.

1. For obvious reasons make absolutely no attempt to communicate with
either the police authorities, or any
private agency. Should you already have
communicated with the police, allow them
to continue their investigation, but do
not mention this letter.

2. Secure before noon today
thousand dollars. (\$10,000.00) This money
must be composed entirely of bills of
the following denominations:
\$2,000.00 in twenty dollar bills
\$8,000.00 in fifty dollar bills
The money must be old. Any attempt to include new or marked bills will render the
entire venture futile.

3. The money should be placed in a
large cigar box, or if this is impossible
in a heavy cardboard box, SECURELY closed
and wrapped in white paper. The wrapping
paper should be sealed at all openings
with sealing wax.

4. Have the money with you prepared
as directed above, and remain at home
after one o'clock P.M. See that the
telephone is not in use.

You will receive a future communication instructing you as to your future
course.

As a final word of warning – this
is a strictly commercial proposition,
and we are prepared to put our threat
into execution should we have reasonable
grounds to believe that you have committed
an infraction of the above instructions.
However, should you carefully follow out
our instructions to the letter, we can
assure you that your son will be safely
returned to you within six hours of our
receipt of the money.

Yours truly,
GEORGE JOHNSON

nday - - 950,621

Chicago THE WORLD'S GREATE

OLUME LXXXIII—NO. 124 C [COPYRIGHT 1924 BY THE CHICAGO TRIBUNE] FRIDAY, MAY 23, 19

KIDNAP RICH B

URT MINUS | NEWS SUMMARY | A WONDERFUL SPRING TO

LE WIND | LOCAL | [Co... Tribune]

(Left) Robert Franks.
(Below) A map of where his body was found.
(Right) A photo of the culvert.

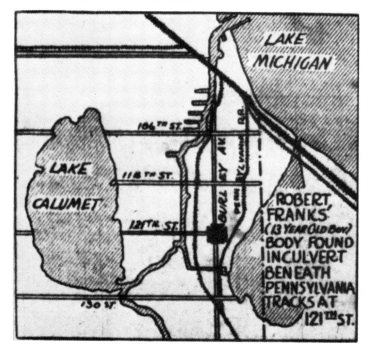

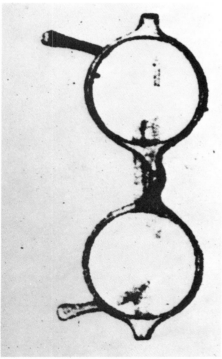

Leopold's automobile and glasses.
Both played a vital role in the case.

student of Friedrich Nietzsche. He wrote to his friend:

"The superman is not liable for anything he may do except for the one crime it is possible for him to commit—to make a mistake."

Perhaps the boys reasoned that if they could indeed commit a major crime without making a mistake, it would validate their claim to super status.

Murder, while satisfying in some respects, was not sufficient in and of itself, the youths decided. Unless there was a motive, the crime would be incomplete. But kidnapping followed by murder and the collection of a ransom—now that was something else. The fact that neither Leopold nor Loeb needed money was dismissed as unimportant. In reality, neither youth could really understand what it would be like to *need* anything material.

As the first step a joint bank account was opened in the names of Morton D. Ballard (Leopold) and Louis Mason (Loeb). In that account they intended to deposit the ransom money. It would also be useful when they rented a car to transport their victim—whoever he should prove to be.

In November 1923, Loeb stole an Underwood typewriter from his fraternity house at Ann Arbor when the two lovers went there, officially, to see a football game. The machine would be used to type the ransom notes.

The new year came and the plans went forward. It was decided to demand that the ransom be placed in a cigar box and that the box be thrown off the three-o'clock train for Michigan City. The problem was to find the right spot. For several weeks they hunted. Leopold knew the area from his bird-watching days, and he designated several places that might be suitable. To make sure, Loeb boarded the train each day and tossed out a cigar-box to Leopold. Finally they found the perfect location.

The next step was to rent the car. "Ballard" did it, giving "Mason" as a reference. The car was left parked at the rental agency, however, to be ready as needed. It was used, for instance, to travel to out-of-way places to buy rope, hydrochloric acid and a few tools. The acid was to be used to destroy the identity of the victim; a learned discussion about the relative merits of hydrochloric versus sulphuric acid occurred before a decision was reached.

Other preparations were made. Both youths obtained loaded pistols. Leopold secured a pair of hip boots for use in a swamp where they planned to hide their victim. A lap robe was included. It would serve to bundle up the body. The ransom note demanding $10,000, was typed and ready.

Only one detail remained—to select their victim.

Loeb's younger brother was considered, but the complications of collecting the ransom saved him. The grandson of Julius Rosenwald, president of Sears, Roebuck and Company, was given serious thought. Finally, they decided to scout the exclusive Harvard Preparatory School, which was close by the Leopold home. Several candidates presumably would suggest themselves.

John Levison was spotted. He seemed ideal, but the boys didn't know his address. After all, one can't deliver a ransom note without an address. They decided to check the telephone book at the local supermarket on the chance his parents had a listed number. They did, but by the time the boys got back, Levison had wandered off. Rather than hunt for him they sought another victim.

Bobby Franks was spotted. He was fourteen and some sort of cousin to Loeb, but nothing close enough to cause complications. Moreover, his father was Jacob Franks, a very wealthy man who wouldn't miss the money.

Being youths of decision, the couple wasted no time. Leopold stopped the car near Bobby and called him over. Bobby knew his relative but something about Leopold repelled him. He declined an offer to "go for a spin." Finally Loeb said he had a new tennis racket and

Shall the trial of Richard Loeb and Nathan Leopold Jr. for the murder of Robert Franks be broadcast by Station W-G-N (formerly WDAP)?

YES ☐   NO ☐

Name ....

Address ....

Please clip this coupon and mail your vote to "Radio," The Chicago Tribune, Tribune Square, Chicago, Ill.

ON TRIAL

During the trial, the *Chicago Tribune* ran the coupon at the top to ask readers if they would like the trial broadcast.
(Below) An editorial cartoon of the day.

Bobby climbed in to hear about it.

Leopold put the car into motion and Loeb immediately stabbed Bobby with a chisel. He had intended to strangle the victim and had a carefully selected bit of rope handy, but Bobby was a little too large for such a method. Instead, he was battered into unconsciousness and permitted to bleed to death as Leopold drove carefully through Chicago traffic on that fine afternoon in May. Loeb wrapped the dying boy in the lap robe but not before a lot of blood spilled out on the car seat.

When it was evident that Bobby was dead, Leopold parked the car and called his father to report he'd be a bit late in getting home that night. Then they ate sandwiches, but the food proved inadequate. Murder was hungry work, they agreed, so they drove to a restaurant and ate a hearty meal. But duty called. It was time to bury the dead.

The spot they selected was near a railroad track where a swamp was bridged by means of a small culvert. The body of ·Bobby Frank was lifted from the car. Acid was splashed over his face and the body was stripped of clothing. Leopold put on his hip boots, picked up the body, and waded into the swamp to the open end of the culvert.

It was dark. The culvert was small and the body didn't slide in easily. Leopold stripped off his coat to give his muscles better play. A pair of horn-rimmed glasses fell out of the coat. They were special glasses of a new type. Only three had been sold in Chicago. But in the blackness, Leopold did not notice them.

He pushed and shoved, and finally the mutilated body slipped into the culvert. But not all the way. One foot remained outside. Again the darkness prevented Leopold from noticing. Besides, he was tired. Next time they would murder a smaller boy.

But the night's work wasn't finished. They drove in their rented car to Indiana and buried Bobby's effects: belt buckle, class ring, and his shoes. With that chore completed, they returned to Chicago. Leopold called the

44

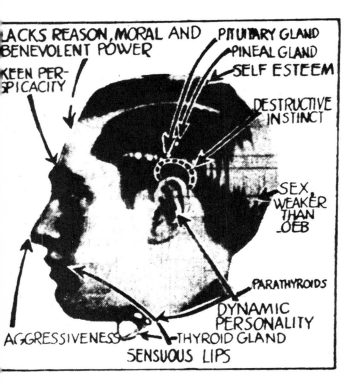

LACKS REASON, MORAL AND BENEVOLENT POWER

PITUITARY GLAND

PINEAL GLAND

SELF ESTEEM

KEEN PER-SPICACITY

DESTRUCTIVE INSTINCT

SEX WEAKER THAN LOEB

PARATHYROIDS

DYNAMIC PERSONALITY

AGGRESSIVENESS

THYROID GLAND

SENSUOUS LIPS

**(Opposite page) Bobby Franks' mother and father during the trial.
(Above) A drawing depicting Leopold's characteristics published in the *Chicago Tribune*.**

(Following page) Darrow (far left) with Loeb (light suit) and Leopold (in front of Loeb and to his right) at the arraignment for murder.

Franks' home. He assured the mother who answered that her son was "safe and unharmed" and would be returned when the ransom was paid. A ransom note giving instructions would arrive next day.

It had been a long day, and so the two friends went to their respective homes and slept the sleep of the unworried. Next day they resumed their chores: they cleaned the blood from the car, they burned the lap robe, they took the stolen typewriter to a park and threw the keys into one lake and the carriage into another.

Meanwhile the first ransom note had been delivered, demanding $10,000 in old, unmarked bills. Small bills—twenties and fifties. The type of bills the youths were accustomed to hand out as tips to waiters who had served them well. The money was supposed to be put in a cigar box and wrapped in white paper. More instructions would follow.

Why didn't the youths give full instructions in the first note? Supremely confident, they enjoyed dragging out the affair. That Jacob Franks would scurry to do their bidding when his son was already dead was a matter of great satisfaction to these would-be supermen.

By the time the youths got around to sending the delivery instructions, their game was lost. A railroad maintenance man spotted the foot of Bobby Franks and called the police. Despite the acid, identification was still possible and within hours newspapers headlined the kidnap-murder of a millionaire's son.

The supermen had made one mistake. Soon others would be revealed.

A great manhunt began. Loeb avidly joined the search, playing private eye and doing his best to divert police with false leads. The cops tolerated him at first because he was another millionaire's son and a distant relative of the dead boy. But when he was overheard remarking that Bobby was "a cocky little son-of-a-bitch," they decided that more than

"MERCY" IS D

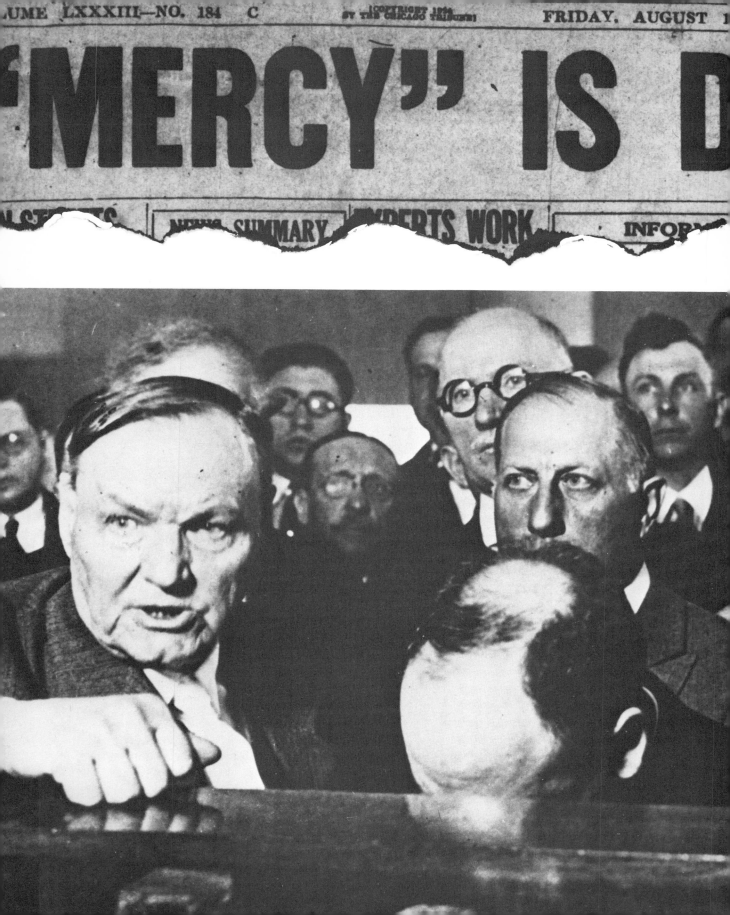

ARROW'S PLEA

WANTED IMMEDIATELY · Hang Slayer, ASSAILS CROWE

Richard Loeb (second from left) and Nathan Leopold (far left) laughing with other young prisoners at the Cook County Jail.

toleration was indicated.

When the glasses were found, Loeb's remark took on sinister implications. For police quickly established that of the three sold in Chicago, one pair had gone to a lawyer who was in Europe at the time of the kidnapping; another had gone to a woman who was wearing them when police interviewed her; and the third had gone to Leopold. Loeb's relationship with Leopold was no secret—at least the superficial aspects of it were known.

Leopold kept his cool, however, when confronted with the glasses. Yes, they were his. He had lost them while bird-watching. Thanks very much for finding them, sir.

But fate was against the supermen. Someone had spotted someone throwing something in the lake the day after the murder. A search, and the typewriter was found. On a hunch, the second lake was dragged and the keys were spotted on the sandy bottom. Then the bloody chisel turned up, and the Leopold family chauffeur recalled he had seen the youths cleaning blood off the seat of a strange automobile.

Desperately Leopold and Loeb tried to establish an alibi. At the time of the kidnapping they were riding around with two girls they had picked up. Where were the girls? How would they know? They had thought they were nice girls, but they were tramps after all.

The press got into the act. Two cub reporters obtained letters Loeb had written. The typing matched the typeface of the stolen typewriter. The reporters were later to win a Pulitzer Prize for their enterprise, since the evidence proved to be the final straw. Loeb broke down and confessed, blaming as much as possible on the "sex pervert" Leopold. The cops played one against the other and soon Leopold was blaming Loeb.

Clarence Darrow, a shaggy bear who often forgot to bathe or shave but never forgot a trick to help a client, was persuaded by Leopold's father to take the case. Reportedly

At right, James Day, twenty-one-year-old convict, entering court to be tried for fatally slashing Richard Loeb.

the fee was to be a million dollars. The canny attorney recognized there was no chance to win acquittal for his clients. If he could save them from execution it would be a miracle. He turned the trial into a battle over the merits of capital punishment.

It became one of the many spectaculars of the 1920's, ranking along with that other courtroom drama, the so-called monkey trial in Dayton, Tennessee, which pitted science against fundamentalism, Darrow against William Jennings Bryan. In impassioned eloquence, Darrow pleaded "for a time when hatred and cruelty will not control the hearts of men, when we can learn by reason and judgment and understanding and faith that all life is worth living and that mercy is the highest attribute of man."

Judge John Caverly, noting that the state had never executed youths of the defendants' ages, sentenced them to ninety-nine years each for kidnapping and to life imprisonment for murder. He also recommended that the two be kept separated for the rest of their lives.

He was ignored. Just as gangsters later learned how to live in prison luxury, so did Leopold and Loeb. They were sent to a state prison outside Joliet, and were given separate cells. But books, desks and filing cabinets were provided each of them. They ate apart from other prisoners in the officer's lounge and their meals were cooked to order. Moreover, they were permitted to visit each other at any time. Together they planted a garden outside the walls and grew flowers. Special food, liquor, drugs were always available and visitors could see them with little trouble. It wasn't a bad life, all in all, especially for two youths who had done just about everything already.

The years passed and inevitably, perhaps, a triangle developed. Late in 1935, Loeb developed a passion for another prisoner. He made advances but was repulsed. Undaunted, he showered the young man with gifts, followed him around and made his life

(Above) News clippings of Loeb's murder while in prison. Nathan Leopold (opposite page, holding his hat, center) is besieged by reporters upon his release from prison.

miserable. Loeb still was accustomed to getting anything he wanted.

The climax came in January 1936. The two men met in the bathroom where Loeb was shaving. A fight began. The other prisoner got the razor and began slashing. Finally Loeb fell to the floor. The prisoner stepped under the shower to wash away the gore while Loeb staggered out of the room to collapse in a corridor. He had been cut more than fifty times and was bleeding to death. Leopold was by his bed when he died a few hours later.

Leopold, with his lover dead, lived on and gradually made adjustments. Three appeals for freedom were denied. His fourth appeal was supported by poet Carl Sandburg who said he would be willing to allow Leopold to live in his home. This time Leopold succeeded. He was paroled on March 13, 1958, and was permitted to fly to Puerto Rico to become a laboratory technician. Three years later he married a widow who owned a flower shop.

Leopold had always loved flowers. He died in 1971.

Let it not be assumed that only the idle sons of the wealthy are inhumane. Four years after Loeb and Leopold attempted their perfect crime and more or less at random snuffed out the life of a human being, an even more horrible act took place in Los Angeles. The man who did it said his sole goal was to get money for a college education. The case caused one contemporary writer to wonder if the most horrible crimes in America "are the work, not of gangsters, but of young men mad about education."

What ever happened to the Know Nothing movement?

Mr. and Mrs. Perry H. Parker were blessed with twin daughters, Marion and Marjorie. In 1928 they were twelve years old and enrolled in junior high school. Perry was a banker and well able to give his children anything within reason. Even a college education, presumably.

Leopold with fiancée, Mrs. Trudi Garcia de Quevado. Photo was taken during a party in honor of Leopold's fifty-sixth birthday.

A family contrast (above, left to right): Marion Parker, her mother and twin sister.
(Below, left to right) Mrs. Hickman, the mother of the accused; William Hickman; his sister Mary and (rear) Mrs. Mary Bright, mother of the youth's former teacher.

The scene as Hickman's death sentence is pronounced. Standing (left to right), Defense Attorney Richard Cantillon, "The Fox," and chief Defense Attorney Jerome Walsh.

William Edward Hickman reading the trial transcript.

On December 18, the twins noticed a strange man lurking outside their home when they left for school. He tried to speak to them but both girls knew better than to encourage him. At noon, however, he appeared at the school and informed authorities that Marion was wanted by her father immediately.

It was the same device used in the Whitla kidnapping, and it worked just as well. The kidnapper used a car instead of a buggy, however, to whisk away his victim. Progress, of a kind, at least.

No one suspected anything until Marjorie came home alone. It didn't take the Parkers long to guess the score. The police were notified, and a search of the city began. Next morning the ransom note arrived by special delivery. It ordered Parker to collect $1,500, in small bills and to wait. The small size of the ransom demand surprised the police, suggesting as it did that the kidnapper was not a professional. It is the amateur who is to be feared in kidnap cases.

Nevertheless, the kidnapper tightened the screws in a professional manner. Although it scarcely was needed, he sent an appeal from Marion. Finally, that night, a telephone message told Parker to take the money to a certain spot. He obeyed, but the police flooded the area and no contact was made.

It was the following afternoon before a new letter was delivered. The kidnapper rebuked Parker for yesterday's failure:

I am vexed and disgusted with you . . . You will never know how you disappointed your daughter . . . Pray to God for forgiveness for your mistake last night.
It was signed: *Fate—Fox*

There was an eloquent little note from Marion included. It read:

Dear Daddy and Mother:
    Daddy, please don't bring any one with you today. I am sorry for what happened last night. We drove right by the house. I cried all the time last night. If you don't meet us this morning, you will never see me again.
              Love to all
              Marion Parker

At 7:15 P.M. the call came. Parker was told

where to go. He was to park his car and turn off the lights. The girl would be waiting. Parker drove to the spot, parked, turned out the lights and waited. A car drove alongside, slowed, moved on. Then it reappeared and stopped beside him. A man pointed a gun and ordered Parker to hand over the money. The father demanded to see the girl. The stranger turned, lifted up the girl's head from beside him. She appeared asleep. Parker assumed she was drugged. He paid the money.

The man drove two hundred feet up the street, stopped, and got out. From the car he lifted the girl's body and placed it on the sidewalk. Then he leaped back into the car and drove away.

Parker ran to his daughter, knelt beside her, and lifted her head. Then he screamed. Her legs were missing—cut off near the hips. The girl was dead—and had been dead for hours.

And all for $1,500.

Los Angeles shared the horror, the shock, the outrage of the Parkers. A reward of $100,000 was offered. By clever detective work, suspicion settled on an eighteen-year-old bank messenger, William Hickman. He denied the crime at first but eventually confessed and added one fact of some value in lessening the horror—Marion had at least been strangled with a towel before her legs were amputated.

Why did he do it? As noted, he wanted to go to college. He went, instead, to Death Row. There was no money to pay for a Clarence Darrow to save him from execution. Crimes are committed by both rich and poor, but assuredly the poor are more apt to pay the penalty. And perhaps that is one reason why organized crime evolves as inevitably as tears.

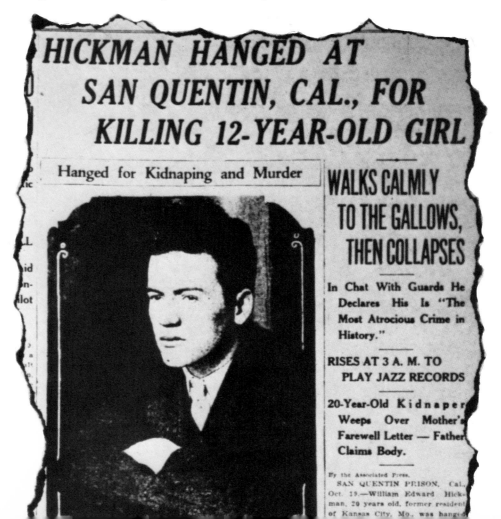

HICKMAN HANGED AT SAN QUENTIN, CAL., FOR KILLING 12-YEAR-OLD GIRL

Hanged for Kidnaping and Murder

WALKS CALMLY TO THE GALLOWS, THEN COLLAPSES

In Chat With Guards He Declares His Is "The Most Atrocious Crime in History."

RISES AT 3 A. M. TO PLAY JAZZ RECORDS

20-Year-Old Kidnaper Weeps Over Mother's Farewell Letter — Father Claims Body.

By the Associated Press.

SAN QUENTIN PRISON, Cal., Oct. 19.—William Edward Hickman, 20 years old, former resident of Kansas City, Mo., was hanged

3. PIGEONS AND THE LINDBERGH EAGLET

Where crime is concerned our thinking often is still influenced by Damon Runyon and his concept of criminals as big-hearted guys and dolls. However, one must judge romantic tales about gangsters with a certain caution, especially if those tales are unsupported, as most of them are, by outside evidence.

Billy Rose, one of America's most successful showmen, got his start with the help of gangsters in the twenties, and in later life enjoyed telling stories about them. One such concerned the love various hard-bitten characters had for racing pigeons which they maintained in coops on the roofs of their ghetto homes. So great did this affection become, according to Rose, that "birdnapping" became common. A prized bird would be stolen and held for ransom. Naturally, such crimes were never reported to police, so no estimate of the size of the ransoms paid are available. What is on record, however, is the number of "accidental deaths" from pigeon-littered roofs. We can only assume that more than one pigeon-napper was properly punished.

Rose went on to tell of the "bum" who was forced to choose between a chorus girl and his pigeons. When he proposed to the girl, she made one condition—the pigeons had to go. On his wedding night the unhappy hood went up on the roof. He picked up four hundred pigeons one at a time, kissed each goodby, and wrung its neck. Gently, of course. So greatly did he prize his beauties he couldn't bear to see them in anyone else's hands. Unfortunately, Rose doesn't tell how long the chorus girl's neck remained unwrung.

It sounds like a great tall story but it may be true, for at least one bird-napping is documented. On March 9, 1974, this all-points bulletin went out to New York City police:

Be on the lookout for 27 racing pigeons believed stolen by a pigeon-napper . . .

Twenty-eight pigeons had been stolen from a Brooklyn roof, police told curious reporters, but one of them was allowed to fly home with the ransom note attached to its leg. "If you want your homer pay $15," the note said.

Because of the small price, police blamed children rather than gangsters for the crime. But a crime *had* occurred.

We begin with a police officer on Staten

A 1927 photo of (left to right)
Ed Diamond, Jack "Legs Diamond"
Noland, "Fatty" Walsh and
"Lucky" Luciano.

58

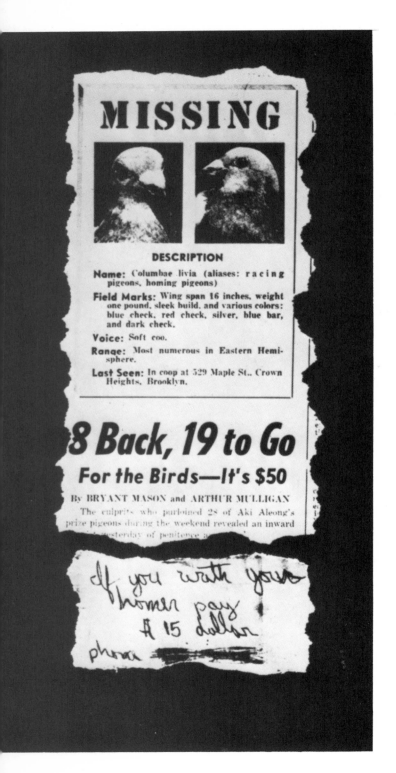

Island on an October day in 1929. He was on duty on Hylan Boulevard when up limped a bloody figure covered with cuts and bruises. The man was expensively dressed and knew what he wanted. He asked the cop to call a taxi.

The officer thought an ambulance would be more appropriate. Despite protests, he called one and sent the walking wounded to the hospital. There detectives questioned him. What was his name?

"Charlie Luciana," was the reluctant reply.

The name was not unknown although it would change to "Luciano" before it became a household word. Here was a minor hood, an "independent" who stood apart from the war then going on in the Mafia between the forces of Joe "the Boss" Masseria and Salvatore Maranzano. It seemed obvious to the detectives that one side or the other had attempted to persuade Luciana that neutrality was becoming dangerous.

"What happened to you?" was the next question.

The patient wasn't too specific. "I was standing on the corner of Fiftieth and Sixth Avenue," he said, "when this car pulls up. Three men get out and put guns on me. They shove me in the car and take off."

Allegedly, they rode around for hours while the kidnappers worked their victim over with fists, feet, and knives. There was some evidence that they had used cigarettes as well. Eventually, Luciana passed out. He woke up on the sands of Huguenot Beach, Staten Island.

Well, what did the kidnappers want?

"Ten thousand dollars," said the gangster. "I told them I'd get it if they'd let me out."

The cops laughed at that one, but the patient stuck to his story. Exactly how he was to pay the ransom when he didn't know the kidnappers, he didn't bother to explain. "Don't worry about it," he told police. "I'll take care of it myself."

Police dusted off an old stolen-car rap and

hung it on Luciana in an effort to detain him, but he quickly posted $25,000 bond and went free. The mystery remained unexplained, but soon cops heard that their ex-patient had a new nickname. For some reason all his friends were calling him "Lucky."

Many years later the "truth" leaked out. It fits known facts very well, and, certainly, the source was in a position to know. But as with any crime story, a self-serving element was involved on the part of the source.

To understand the later version it is necessary to know more about the Mafia civil war than did the police of the period.

Masseria was the official *Capo dei Capi Re*, or boss of all the bosses. In reality, the various Mafia "families" were largely autonomous, but lip-service was still paid to the idea of a national organization. The *Capo dei Capi Re* was supposed to settle disputes between individual bosses, and otherwise provide some coordination so that a Mafioso from New York would feel welcome in Chicago or Denver. In reality he spent most of his time conspiring to knock off his rivals. One such rival was Maranzano, who had challenged Masseria and made it stick. Luciana was, nominally, a lieutenant of Masseria. In reality, he had secretly allied himself with various "Young Americans" in the Mafia—men who were fed up with the way the "Mustache Petes" of the organization neglected business to pursue old-country vendettas. More important, he had joined forces with Meyer Lansky, who was attempting to build a "combination" of all ethnic groups—including those of Italian descent. Luciana was important to Lansky's future plans and, aware of the danger to his buddy, Lansky had placed him under the protection of his own Bugs and Meyer mob. Within minutes after Luciana was shoved into that car at Fiftieth and Sixth Avenue, Lansky knew of it and had men searching. The car was located and followed. Bugsy Siegel was in command. But Lansky was curious as to what the kidnappers' motives were and he gave

Julian "Babe" Jones who pleaded guilty to kidnapping James Hackett, the wealthy Illinois gambler, in Chicago.

orders to the impatient Siegel to wait.

Hours passed and the black car with drawn curtains drove discreetly around the streets of New York. Then came the message from Siegel—a man had left the kidnap car and entered another car alongside it. Presumably it was Maranzano—finished with his interview of Luciana. Now the car containing Luciana was moving faster—and was headed for the ferry to Staten Island.

Lansky gave orders and left in his own car for the scene. The action was over when he arrived. Siegel had cut off the mystery car, which had tried to escape by driving across a parking lot. Another of Siegel's men was there to block the exit. A quick burst of gunfire, and the kidnappers were dead. Luciana was alive, but in sad condition. He had been tortured to make him talk.

Now he gasped out the information he was later to refuse police. "Maranzano," he said. "He wanted me to tell him where to find Joe the Boss."

Lansky wasted no time. It was imperative that Maranzano and Masseria be kept in ignorance of the "third force" which Luciana and Lansky had formed. The murder of three men couldn't be concealed but the circumstances could be made into a mystery. He gave orders to take the bodies to New Jersey and dump them. Luciana was to be taken to Staten Island. Let the cops find him in a dazed condition. Maranzano might suspect things weren't kosher, but he'd never figure out the truth.

Luciana protested: "Nobody'll believe I got taken for a ride and lived."

"You're just lucky, I guess," said Meyer Lansky.

And that is the version that has survived Lucky Luciano and is told today when old-timers discuss the games of their youth.

Sure to be mentioned in any such discussions is James Hackett who broke the

Arthur Palumbo, Peter Coll, Lottie Kriesberger and Vincent "Mad Dog" Coll.

underworld code and called in police. Much good it did him.

Hackett was a gambling-house operator in Chicago, something of an independent. He had had trouble with Al Capone and with the other gangs who fought with Capone for control of the Windy City. When Hackett refused to cut in some extra partners in his gambling joint, someone decided to teach him a lesson. They could have wrecked the place, of course, or blown it up, but such violent action was not productive. Instead, they invaded a golf course on which he was playing with his six-year-old son. Producing a battery of revolvers and machine guns, they offered Hackett a choice—either he or his son could go along as hostage for payment of $150,000 ransom.

It was quite a sum—the largest ever paid up until that time. And why was it so large? The kidnappers had a double purpose. By stripping the gambler of his roll, so to speak, they made it necessary for him to accept partners in his gambling house.

Some rather drastic persuasion was required before Hackett consented to write instructions to his wife to convert jewelry and securities into cash. She obeyed, and the 57-year-old man was released unharmed. Why not, since he couldn't recognize anyone and they needed him to run his gambling joint for them.

Hackett was unreconciled. Angry, he went to the police with the story. His action was one of the very few times that details of an underworld kidnapping got on the official police blotter.

The cops listened, made unhappy noises, and promised to investigate. Only then did it dawn on Hackett—a slow learner, apparently—that organized crime was supreme in Cook County, Illinois. Most of the time, anyway. A sadder and wiser man, Hackett went back to his gambling joint to meet his new partners.

However, no one ever told the cops the truth

about the kidnapping of "Big Frenchy"
DeMange, chief of staff to Owney "the Killer"
Madden. It was done by Vincent "Mad Dog"
Coll, a man who dared do anything. Big
Frenchy was allegedly taken to a house in
White Plains, New York, where Coll—again
allegedly—stuck lighted matches under his toe
nails until the gangster expressed a desire to go
home. He was allowed to talk to his friend and
boss, Owney, and convey his sentiments.
Owney, a compassionate fellow according to
his obituary some forty years later, ransomed
his lieutenant for anywhere from twenty to
fifty thousand dollars. Accounts vary,
depending upon which gangster you listen to.

Rumor has it that Coll was so pleased with
his coup, he decided to snatch the old master
himself. But someone was too smart. Coll was
lured into a telephone booth in a drugstore
near Madden's home. He was listening so hard
he didn't see the machine gunner who stepped
into the drugstore, pulled his weapon out from
beneath his coat, and cut Coll to pieces before
the "Mad Dog" could hang up.

The Kefauver Committee in 1951 heard
more about the Big Frenchy-Madden
relationship. A witness told of a 1932 gangster
convention at Atlantic City, New Jersey. At
the banquet session, Big Frenchy was to make
a presentation to Owney. He called him up to
the podium and said:

"Owney, have you got a watch?"

Owney said he did and produced it. Big
Frenchy reached for it, then dropped it.
Carefully he stepped forward and ground it
beneath his feet.

"Gee, I'm sorry," said Big Frenchy, "but
here's another one for you."

And he presented him with a special
engraved one that cost thousands.

One could tell other stories about
kidnapping. During the 1920's no gangster or
gangster-related show business personality was
safe from kidnappers. Even such a celebrity as
Texas Guinan of "Hello, sucker" fame drove
around in a bullet-proof car which was

Texas Guinan getting religion as she
prepares to join Aimee Semple
McPherson's temple.
(Opposite page) Frenchy DeMange.

Lindbergh with the Spirit of St. Louis
(opposite page).
(Below) A song commemorating
his flight.

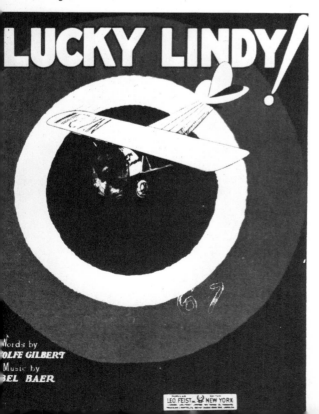

LUCKY LINDY!

Words by
WOLFE GILBERT
Music by
ABEL BAER

LEO. FEIST · NEW YORK

rumored to have once belonged to a king. Word spread around the grapevine one night that she was scheduled to be "snatched." Preventive measures were quickly taken to convince the would-be kidnappers that Texas was off-limits. Reportedly, it was necessary to kill a man to get the message across.

The aftermath of a kidnapping brought down John T. Noland, the infamous "Legs Diamond" of the Prohibition era, who cheated death and the law for many years. An outlaw's outlaw, he worked for Arnold Rothstein, for Lansky, for Costello and for Dutch Schultz until he had no friends left. But because he was dangerous the underworld hesitated about taking him on. For a brief period it looked as if the law might eliminate the problem. Legs was indicted for kidnapping a cider-hauler, one James Duncan. He came to trial in upstate New York and to everyone's amazement was acquitted. That night as he celebrated with his girl friend, the underworld sent a team of killers to meet him. Legs was quite dead when found.

And so it went during the "Roaring Twenties" and very early thirties. When gangster kidnapped gangster, who gave a damn? It was, as previously noted, the era of the "Lost Generation," of the "new look" in crime, women, sports, and morals. An easy cynicism was in style, a cynicism based not on painfully acquired understanding of things as they are, but on ballyhoo and a philosophy of easy virtue. Sensations came and went quickly but no matter since tomorrow would bring something new.

A sensation of the thirties that endured was a young man named Charles A. Lindbergh, who on May 19, 1927, climbed into a tiny little plane at Roosevelt Field outside New York and took off in the rain for Paris.

As word flashed around the country by telegraph and telephone that "Lucky Lindy"—so dubbed by reporters before his flight—was in the air, the entire population began rooting for him. At a heavyweight championship fight

2 CENTS
PAY NO MORE!

Chicago
THE WORLD'S

VOLUME LXXXXI.—NO. 53 C   [REG. U.S. PAT. OFFICE. COPYRIGHT 1932 BY THE CHICAGO TRIBUNE.]   WEDNESDAY. MARCH

LINDBERGH B

SCHOOL SAVING | **NEWS SUMMARY** | **CHINESE LINES**

ily **Tribune**

TEST NEWSPAPER

932.—28 PAGES   THIS PAPER CONSISTS OF TWO SECTIONS—SECTION ONE   ★★★★   PRICE TWO CENTS   IN CHICAGO AND SUBURBS   ELSEWHERE THREE CENTS

BY IS STOLEN

OUR JONAH

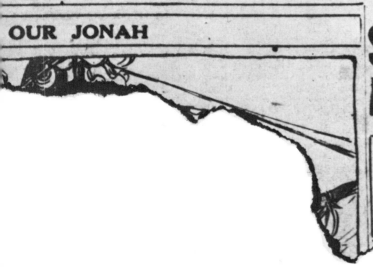

SEIZED WHILE SLEEPING I[N] HOME AT HOPEWELL, N. J[.]

COLONEL TELLS KNOWN DETAILS OF HIS LOSS

LETIN.
March

Troops and Police
Many States Join
in the Search.

(Opposite page) Charles A. Lindbergh, Jr., during celebration of his first birthday. (Left) The Lindbergh home flooded with reporters and investigators. A search plane overhead.

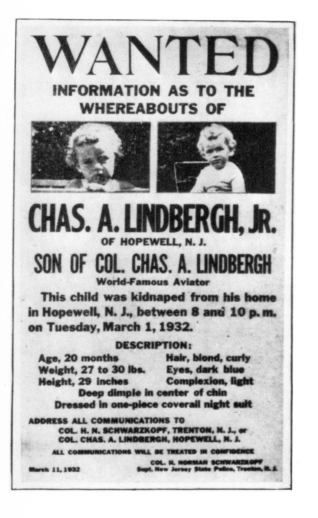

WANTED

INFORMATION AS TO THE
WHEREABOUTS OF

CHAS. A. LINDBERGH, Jr.
OF HOPEWELL, N. J.

SON OF COL. CHAS. A. LINDBERGH
World-Famous Aviator

This child was kidnaped from his home
in Hopewell, N. J., between 8 and 10 p. m.
on Tuesday, March 1, 1932.

DESCRIPTION:

Age, 20 months	Hair, blond, curly
Weight, 27 to 30 lbs.	Eyes, dark blue
Height, 29 inches	Complexion, light

Deep dimple in center of chin
Dressed in one-piece coverall night suit

ADDRESS ALL COMMUNICATIONS TO
COL. H. N. SCHWARZKOPF, TRENTON, N. J., or
COL. CHAS. A. LINDBERGH, HOPEWELL, N. J.

ALL COMMUNICATIONS WILL BE TREATED IN CONFIDENCE

COL. H. NORMAN SCHWARZKOPF
March 11, 1932   Supt. New Jersey State Police, Trenton, N. J.

on May 20, some forty thousand fans including the cream of the underworld stood for a minute in silent prayer for the "Lone Eagle." When news of his landing in Paris came in, it caused the biggest celebration, the most genuine outpouring of pride and joy since the Armistice of 1918.

When reports arrived describing his modest behavior in Paris, he quickly slipped into super star status. He became a Hero, and a Hero was something new to a generation which had accepted Babe Ruth, Jack Dempsey, and Cautious Cal as representative of the best the country offered. Lindbergh came home to a wild reception—came home on a cruiser sent by President Coolidge. The ticker tape parade down Broadway set a record, with eighteen-hundred tons of paper fluttering to the street. The young man was commissioned a colonel, given more decorations than he could wear, and offered millions in various promotional stunts, which he turned down.

Surprisingly, the glory did not seem to change the hero. He remained modest, somewhat shy, and dignified. He married Anne Morrow, daughter of the ambassador to Mexico. They settled down near Hopewell, New Jersey, and in time a son was born. The parents called him Charles A. Lindbergh, Jr., but the press referred to him as the "Little Eaglet." If possible, his father became even more beloved by millions who never tired of reading about him. As Frederick Lewis Allen put it in his book, *Only Yesterday,* "Lindbergh was a god."

So it was with a real sense of shock that the American people learned on March 2, 1932, that Lindbergh's baby had been kidnapped.

It happened in the night. Early in the evening Mrs. Lindbergh and Betty Gow, the baby's nurse, put the infant to bed. The nurse did not leave his room until she was sure he was asleep. A little later Lindbergh heard a noise and mentioned it to his wife. But the noise was not repeated and so it was ignored. Only the howl of the March wind around the isolated house continued.

St. Raymond's Cemetery, Bronx, New York City. White cross is where Hauptmann sprang over the fence to meet Dr. John F. Condon, called "Jafsie," who handed the $50,000 ransom to him where the hedge is marked with an "X" on the right.

An hour after the noise was heard, the nurse made her usual check of the nursery. The baby was gone. Frantically the Lindberghs began looking. The baby had just begun to walk; it was conceivable, perhaps, that he had climbed out of his bed and tottered off. But he could not be found. Outside the window of the nursery a home-made ladder was found, with one rung broken. Near the window sill was a note that in somewhat broken English ordered:

Have fifty thousand dollars ready, 25,000 in twenty-dollar bills 15,000 in ten-dollar bills, and 10,000 in five-dollar bills. In 4–5 days we will inform you where to deliver the money. We warn you for making anyding public or for notify the police The child is in gut care Indication for all letters are signature and three holes.

But the police had been called even before the note was found, and soon the word was out to the press and to the country. Lindbergh wanted above all to recover his baby. He was willing to cooperate with anyone, including the kidnapper. And that became a problem. For everyone in the country, it seemed, except the kidnapper, wanted to cooperate with Lindbergh in solving the "crime of the century." Everybody tried to get into the act and too many succeeded. The investigation became a crime circus with no one daring to take charge and run it properly. Lindbergh was too much of a celebrity. His wishes came first, and, while a great pilot, he was not an investigator.

The initial assumption was that the crime had to be the work of the organized underworld. No independent operator would have dared to try such a shocking caper, it was felt. Only the depraved would even *want* to steal the Lone Eagle's son.

On March 10, 1932, Arthur Brisbane, a highly paid columnist-spokesman for William Randolph Hearst and his newspaper empire, informed the nation that if Al Capone were freed from prison he would try to find the baby and restore him to the arms of his mother.

Capone had only recently been convicted of income tax evasion and sent to prison. He was naturally quite eager to get out. Built up by the press as the leading gangster of the nation, it seemed logical that if, as assumed, the underworld had stolen the baby, Capone could find it. Logical, of course, if one remembers that no one knew much about organized crime in those days despite the millions of words that

Al Capone (left) offered his services
in solving the kidnapping.
(Opposite page) Several underworld
figures offered their services, including
Pat Crowe, the kidnapper of young
Edward Cudahy.

had been written and read. No federal agency existed to keep track of criminals, and certainly there was no system whereby individual cities could obtain information. The Internal Revenue Service had a special intelligence unit to catch tax evaders and of late it had been used primarily against gangsters. Yet such probes were always on a specific case basis and there was no real understanding of the national alliances that even then were bringing the future syndicate into being.

Columnist Brisbane, having settled a tax case for approximately $250,000, obviously didn't consider Capone's crime a serious one when compared to the necessity of finding a missing child. And such was the influence of the Hearst press that many were impressed with his logic. Among those was Colonel Lindbergh.

The day after Brisbane's suggestion about Capone, A.P. Madden, special agent in

Chicago for the I.R.S. and one of the men who had made the tax case against Capone, wrote a long personal letter to his boss, Elmer Irey, in Washington. The letter indicated that a well organized campaign to free Capone was already under way even before Brisbane's column. Madden wrote in part:

Several days ago, when some members of the Capone organization concluded that Al Capone might be helped through a solution of the Lindbergh kidnapping, a determined effort was made to locate (Robert) Conroy. I am advised that an ex-convict operates a florist shop on South Michigan Avenue. That location is a congregating place for criminals affiliated with the Capones. The telephone numbers are given as Wabash 0579 and Wabash 0580. I am told that these phones were, and perhaps are, being used for local and long distance calls in an effort to ascertain the whereabouts of Conroy . . . I know that Frank Rio, one of Capone's principal lieutenants, has been trying to find Conroy from another location. It is said that Rio is communicating with Capone in

Sun

★★★★

BID AND ASKED PRICES

MARCH 11, 1932.

PRICE THREE CENTS.

UNDERWORLD LEADERS SEEK CREDIT IN LINDBERGH CASE

Spitale and Bitz in U. S. Court

Indicted Under Assumed Names in Connection With Seizure of Liquor in Brooklyn.

Salvatore Spitale and Irving Bitz, the two reputed underworld characters designated by Col. Charles A. Lindbergh to negotiate with the kidnapers of his baby, were positively identified today as two of sixteen men on trial in the Federal Court in Brooklyn on charges of conspiracy to violate the prohibition law.

The identification was made for reporters by Abraham Kesselman, attorney for the two men. Spitale was indicted under the name of James Martin of 240 East Thirteenth street, Manhattan, and Bitz, his right hand man, was indicted under the

Cannot Bar Teachers Because of Religion

ALBANY, March 11 (U. P.).—The Hayes bill, prohibiting school superintendents from inquiring the religion of teachers applying for jobs,

HEADS LINDBERGH SEARCH

Col. Norman Schwarzkopf.

arch Is Fruitless

Owney Madden Joins Ranks of Those Who Say They Are Seeking Baby.

AL CAPONE IS ALSO IN LINE

Belief Spreads That Spitale and Bitz Suggested Themselves to Child's Father.

This is the tenth day since the Lindbergh baby was kidnaped and there are no indications that his return is imminent, although there is reason to believe that Col. Charles A. Lindbergh is indirectly in communication with the kidnapers.

The most obvious development is the benevolent intervention of the underworld. It almost begins to look as if there were a concerted movement on the part of reputed and racketeers on the Lindbergh whatever there is ward, and particude.

New York's new who is, in with the Parole Capone and a Mor Spitale and Irving service to re

Capone's Offer to Lindy Stirs Bingham; Demands Dry Repeal

[Chicago Tribune Press Service.]

Washington, D. C., April 23.—[Special.]—Prohibition produced the bootleg racket. The racket produced Al Capone. Capone and his kind stepped crime up to a new daring which reached a climax in the kidnaping of the Lindbergh baby. In these three steps Senator Bingham [Reg. Conn.] today outlined to the senate what he believes to be the sequence of the 18th amendment which he seeks to have repealed.

Then he took three parallel steps based on repeal.

The abolishment of prohibition will, he predicted, take the profit out of the bootleg racket. This will strip power from the gangster. This, in turn, will reduce crime.

Links Dry Law to Kidnaping.

Senator Bingham pointed out that he did not specifically blame the Lindbergh kidnaping on prohibition, but he argued the connection in this way:

new crime and I do not belie been caused by prohibition same time it must be obviou one that the successful ha crime on a large scale ha ably been due to the e of bootleggers."

Calling attention to of this morning wh Capone had not only guaranteed, to get the back, if given oppor Bingham said that inc cient to show the pow gangland.

HIRAM BINGHAM.

Detroit Purple Gang Sought

Connection Seen With Kidnaping of Lindbergh Baby—Raids Made in Chicago.

DETROIT, March 4 (A. P.).—The Detroit police today worked on what New Jersey authorities thought might be a local angle of the Lindbergh kidnaping. The investigation was started last night after a long telephone conversation between a Newark, N. J., detective, and of the Detroit police.

SPEED IS URGED BY EX-KIDNAPER

Pat Crowe, Abductor of Cudahy, Gives Advice.

Recommendations from a man who formerly made a business of kidnaping were added today to the many suggestions received from all quarters by officials working on the Lindbergh case.

From Scranton, Pa., Pat Crowe, who achieved nationwide notoriety when he kidnaped Edward Cudahy in 1900, offered the following advice to Col. and Mrs. Lindbergh through the United Press:

"Pay the kidnapers anything they demand, be it million.

ter bore a Yorktown anniversary stamp none of which was sold in Schuylkill county.

Postcard From Dover.

DOVER, N. J.—A postcard, addressed to Col. Charles A. Lindbergh, bearing the message, "Discontinue search. Baby safe," was mailed here today.

The card was turned over to Chief of Police Charles Counterman who immediately organized a party to search boarding and rooming houses in the district.

Trace Milk Bottle Caps.

NEWARK, Ohio.—Police of this town found two milk bottles, one bearing a New Jersey company cap, the other a Pennsylvania cap, near the main road from Granville, Ohio. This was considered of some significance in light of the letter intercepted at Granville which said: "Tell Ann not to be nervous, everything O. K. Give us time."

(Top) Elmer L. Irey.
(Below) Owney Madden.

jail, in spite of the guards that have been placed there by the United States Marshal, and all the indications are that Capone himself has concluded that Conroy is a very promising prospect.

I am sending a photograph of Conroy, herewith. I am told that the photograph is an excellent likeness except that when Conroy was here last summer he looked somewhat heavier than he appears to be in the photograph.

I am advised that there is a man in the East, presumably a New York Italian, named Charles Lucky (spelling of last name uncertain) who has more influence among the criminal Italians than Al Capone ever had. It is said that Lucky is Capone's boss and the boss of all the other Italians engaged in important violations of the law. The thought was expressed that Lucky, in view of his great influence, could do more in the Lindbergh kidnapping case, if anything could be done at all, than Capone could do. I do not recall that I ever heard of Lucky, but I presume that he is as influential as he is reported to be. If this particular kidnapping is an underworld crime, perhaps means could be devised to communicate with Lucky and to get his cooperation if that has not already been done . . .

The "Charles Lucky" referred to was, of course, Lucky Luciano, as he now called himself. He was not contacted in the Lindbergh case, as far as is known, but a decade later Naval intelligence sought his help in putting the Mafia on the side of the good guys in World War II. The Robert Conroy mentioned was identified elsewhere in the letter as one of those believed to have taken part in the St. Valentine's Day massacre of Capone's enemies. Madden noted that Conroy "is a man who can adjust himself to almost any conditions" and, in addition, "he makes a very good appearance . . . and is much given to reading good literature."

Armed with his aide's letter, the I.R.S. intelligence boss, Elmer Irey, was prepared when the inevitable order came from his boss, Secretary of the Treasury Ogden Mills. Irey was told to go to Hopewell and discuss Capone's offer, transmitted via Brisbane, with Lindbergh. He persuaded the desperate aviator

Colonel Charles A. Lindbergh and his
attorney, Harry Breckenridge.

that Al's high-sounding plea was just a
gimmick to get out of jail. Irey promised that,
acting unofficially, he would do everything
Capone could do and more. Lindbergh was
impressed.

Madden and a colleague, Frank J. Wilson,
who would soon become head of the Secret
Service, were ordered to New York from
Chicago to find Conroy. Mike Malone, the
agency's star undercover man, was also
assigned. They were quietly digging away
when, on May 11, a new convulsion shook the
nation. On that day a body identified as the
Lindbergh baby was found near Hopewell.
Hysteria mounted. President Herbert Hoover
ordered all government agencies having
investigators to cooperate with New Jersey
which had prime jurisdiction. Secretary Mills
ordered Irey to cooperate and added:

The three government departments having
investigation services should at once coordinate
themselves under the direction of the Department of
Justice and through this agency offer themselves to
assist the police of New Jersey in every possible
way. You will, accordingly, see that insofar as your
Bureau is concerned, this case is treated as a live
one for an indefinite period. You will further get in
touch with Mr. Hoover of the Department of
Justice, who is charged with responsibility of
coordinating the activities of the Federal services.

A good soldier, Irey obeyed. John E.
Hoover, as he was then known, said he was
assigning one of his special agents to act as
liaison officer between his office and the state
police. All other federal agents working the
case were to be withdrawn.

Reluctantly, Irey told Madden and Wilson
they were off the case. Madden went back to
Chicago while Wilson went on vacation. When
Lindbergh learned of this he raised hell.
Signals were changed immediately. It took a
conference with President Hoover to settle
things, but the upshot of it was that the I.R.S.
men went back to work and the F.B.I. man
was withdrawn.*

Upon returning, Irey's men were shocked to
be introduced to three bona fide gangsters who

*It should be noted that neither the I.R.S. nor the F.B.I.
existed as agencies with those initials in 1932, but in the
interests of easy reading the identification recognized today is
used.

Arthur P. Madden (seated, center) and Frank Wilson (standing), investigators for the I.R.S., assisting New Jersey authorities in investigating the Lindbergh case.

had been invited aboard by Colonel Lindbergh. Two of them were relatively minor league, Salvatore Spitale and Irving Bitz, but the third was none other than that recent recipient of a gold watch, Owney "the Killer" Madden. Obviously, Lindbergh was leaving no stone unturned, regardless of what might be crawling beneath it.

Owney the Killer was unique in underworld circles—a W.A.S.P. Born in England, he grew up in New York where as boss of the Gophers he gained a reputation long before World War I. Police credited him with five murders before they sent him to prison. He got out in 1923 and became a rumrunner of note, the owner of nightclubs, and the secret owner of heavyweight champion Primo Carnera. Too independent to join the "Combination" in the latter stages of Prohibition, Owney hoped his services to Lindbergh would help maintain his position in New York.

Madden of the I.R.S.—no relation to Owney —accepted the situation. Owney and undercover man Mike Malone were assigned to penetrate a spiritualist church and make contact with the spirits. The assignment resulted from an episode in which Colonel Henry Breckinridge, Lindbergh's chief adviser, was called to Somerset, New Jersey, by a couple promising information. While the distinguished Breckinridge watched, the woman went into a trance and moaned aloud that the ransom note had been left near the window. Since this had not been published, it appeared significant. The medium, who called herself Mary Magdalene, then told Breckinridge to visit his office next morning for important information. He was impressed enough to do so, and even more impressed when a new ransom note arrived there. Since Owney had sent a lot of men to the spirit world, it was presumed he might have influence there. Unhappily, he was unable to make contact with them and the probe ended in a blank.

Shortly thereafter Owney went into exile in Hot Springs, Arkansas. He married the postmaster's daughter and settled down to running a tightly controlled miniature gambling empire. Strictly illegal, it nevertheless flourished for more than thirty years. Hot Springs became a hiding place for syndicate gangsters. When Luciano was arrested there a few years later, it was almost necessary to call up the national guard to get him out.

Another gangster who got favorable attention in the Lindbergh kidnapping case was Abner "Longie" Zwillman, the so-called Al Capone of New Jersey. Zwillman was in charge of getting the "Big Seven's" liquor convoys from shore to warehouse, and the concentration of investigative authority in the Hopewell area began to complicate his task. He offered a huge reward for the kidnapper, and the public applauded his public spirit.

Meanwhile, Madden of the I.R.S. had not forgotten that Capone's candidate was Robert Conroy. The search begun by Capone's men was continued by the I.R.S. Eventually, his trail was found. I.R.S. men in Miami discovered that Conroy and a blonde had spent some time in the Magic City—it was, after all, Capone's favorite retreat as well—before the kidnapping. New York was supposed to have been his destination, but no trace of him surfaced until August 1932. Then a couple was found dead in an apartment near Broadway on West 102nd Street. Police identified the bodies as Robert and Rosemary Sanford, and called the deaths a murder-suicide. The man had apparently shot the woman and then himself. A counterfeiting plant was found in the apartment along with some good-quality counterfeit money.

Madden and Wilson became interested when their sources in the Capone mob whispered that Conroy was dead. Then came an anonymous note:

Longie Zwillman.

Check activities of Robert and Rosemary Sanford in Lindbergh case. Keep quiet until convinced. 221.

The fingerprints of Robert Sanford were checked against those on file for Robert Conroy. They matched. Sanford was Conroy, but what had that to do with the Lindbergh kidnapping? It was to remain one of the many unsolved mysteries surrounding the Lindbergh case. Years later, there was speculation the Capone gang had intended to pin the kidnapping on Conroy, and take the credit for solving the case even if they had to frame Conroy to do it. If so, what went wrong? Not even the old-timers who like to speak with seeming authority about the past profess to have the answer to that one.

While the hunt for Conroy was pursued, investigators were following another strange trail. The tip came from Detroit, where an informant whispered that the kidnapper was Waslov Simek who, earlier, had been convicted of extortion for threatening to kidnap Edsel Ford's baby. Upon his release from prison in 1925, he had been deported to his native Czechoslovakia. But he might have returned.

Excitement mounted when Dr. John F. Condon, the self-appointed intermediary in the case, almost identified Simek as the man he had passed the ransom money to. He picked Simek's picture out of a file and said: "Boys, you're hot. I want to see that man."

The trail seemed to get hotter still as the probe went on. It was learned that Simek had gotten into trouble in Czechoslovakia and fled the country after being charged with arson. He went to Russia where history repeated itself. Patiently the I.R.S. reconstructed his itinerary further: India, South America, and then, in 1931, Santo Domingo in the Caribbean.

There a dead end. For in Santo Domingo, Simek found employment with a public service corporation. His job was to read certain instruments each day and to make written reports. Such reports were found for the day of the kidnapping.

Was it a coincidence then that some months

The famous ladder and the matching piece of flooring which was found in the Hauptmann home.
(Right) Bruno Richard Hauptmann, the accused.

later a cablegram should arrive from the United States consul in Budapest, Hungary, asking if there was any doubt that the body found near Hopewell was the Lindbergh child? If any doubt existed, the consul continued, an investigation should be made in the town of Uzsok across the border in Czechoslovakia. Hungarian police insisted that the Lindbergh baby was there.

Although the body found near Hopewell had been badly decomposed, Colonel Lindbergh had identified it as his son. So long as he remained certain, no one was going to question the identification despite Simek and the American consul in Budapest. The matter was dropped. The arrest of Bruno Richard Hauptmann on September 19, 1934, seemed to wrap things up. The key to his arrest was a marked bill which had been included in the ransom at the insistence of the I.R.S. In Hauptmann's house was found $14,600 of the ransom money.

Hauptmann persisted in declaring his innocence. A case of circumstantial evidence was built that convinced a jury and most persons acquainted with details. But such was the public interest in all things pertaining to Lindbergh that doubts remained. Even Harold Hoffman, governor of New Jersey, was far from satisfied. He delayed the execution of Hauptmann long enough to investigate a phony "confession"—just one of the many subplots that confused investigators.

Hauptmann was electrocuted on April 3, 1936. The nation had been given a play-by-play account of the trial by radio, and now it listened in fascinated horror as Gabriel Heatter ad-libbed for hours while waiting for the lights to dim in the prison at Trenton. Ironically, Heatter was later to be remembered for his work during World War II when he began each broadcast with the declaration: "There's good news tonight, folks."

The doubts remained after Hauptmann's death. In 1973, various authors received packets of documents purporting to prove that one Harold Olson of Westport, Connecticut, was really Charles A. Lindbergh, Jr. The material was, of course, persuasive, but proof was lacking. Like so many other events in the Lindbergh case, it resembled a story one aging underworld character might tell another as they sit in a cabana on Miami Beach and sip tall drinks while waiting for the sunset.

VOLUME XCV.—NO. 82 C   SATURDAY. APRIL 4, 1936.— PAGES   PRICE TWO CENTS

HAUPTMANN PUT TO DEAT

ATTLE RAGES | NEWS SUMMARY | JURORS ACQUIT | WHEN THE SUN FINALLY COMES UP | CALM UNBROKEN AS HE STEPS TO ELECTRIC CHAIR

Hope for Reprieve Is Held to Last.

"POOR RIC IS WIDOW'S FLASH OF

4. THE F.B.I. BUILDS A LEGEND

The arrest and subsequent conviction of Bruno Hauptmann for the Lindbergh kidnapping did not kill the popular legend that organized crime had turned to the "snatch racket" on a big scale.

Prohibition was on its last legs in 1932. It seemed obvious to many law-enforcement officials that the "liquor gangs" would turn to a new field of enterprise. What then was more likely than kidnapping? The correct answer was organized gambling, but it took some years for that to become clear.

Writers, needing as always someone to quote, were happy to give these total guess work views vast publicity. Consequently an amazing amount of nonsense was published and presumably believed by a public which if possible knew even less about what was going on than the writers and the cops.

One author, in a book written in 1932 after the Lindbergh kidnapping, discussed at great length the various "kidnapper syndicates" said to be operating. "The first big band of kidnapper specialists," he wrote, was organized in Detroit which "thus claims the dubious

fame of being the 'kidnapper capital' of the United States." The name of this first kidnapper syndicate? "The Purple Gang," according to the author.

This statement is so inaccurate as to be almost funny. There was a Purple Gang of Detroit, which had begun as an ethnic street gang in the Jewish ghetto of the city. It preyed on local shopkeepers. The name, one of the most enduring in the annals of modern crime, was coined by an angry shopkeeper one day after his business establishment had been vandalized. "That bunch is off-color," he remarked to a sympathetic neighbor. "Yeah," said the neighbor, "they're purple. They're the purple gang." A reporter quoted the comment and the name was born. With the coming of Prohibition, the youths went into rum-running across Lake Erie and soon built up a thriving business. They had several wars with rival gangs and were forced to import Italian killers from St. Louis for use as "muscle." All this was ancient history at the time the 1932 book was written, and was known to every crime reporter in Detroit.

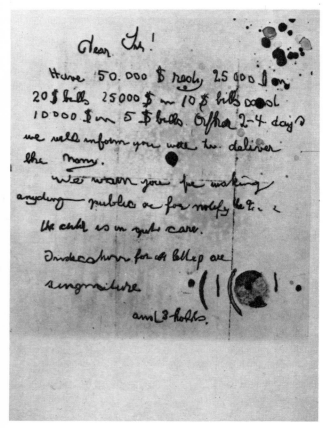

The Lindbergh ransom note, left by
the kidnapper at the scene of the crime.

The attitude of such irresponsible crime writers was well demonstrated by Stanley Walker, city editor of the New York *Herald Tribune,* in his book, *The Night Club Era.* Speaking of kidnap gangs, Walker wrote: "There are some lurid tales of these organizations, but none too lurid to be believed."

Walker went on to explain his theory of the makeup of such gangs. Most important, he said, was "the Peddler," whose sole role was to tell the gang who could be most profitably kidnapped. Presumably such a man knew how to read the newspapers.

Then came "the Finger," a brainy chap who learned all there is to know about the target: "his personal habits, his bank accounts, his business deals, his servants, the arrangement of his home, his peculiar weaknesses if any, and everything else that may be useful." Quite an assignment. A man with that ability should have been made police chief.

"The Spotter" was the leader of the gang on the actual snatch. His principal requirement was nerve. And intelligence. This last was an important admission. Ordinarily, it was the habit of the period to describe all gangsters as "rats" lacking either intelligence or compassion. J. Edgar Hoover set the style.

Once the snatch had been made, "the Voice" took over. He had to arrange the payment of the ransom and make sure no trap had been set. According to Walker, "this man gets a large share of whatever money is collected, for his is a ticklish role."

Confronted with this cast of specialists, one has to wonder how the old-timers had the nerve to attempt the crime back in the buggy days.

One result of the public uproar over the Lindbergh kidnapping and the publicity about the "new menace" was the passage of the so-called Lindbergh Law. It enabled the F.B.I. to enter cases where state lines had been crossed or, in the absence of evidence to the contrary, when it was *presumed* such

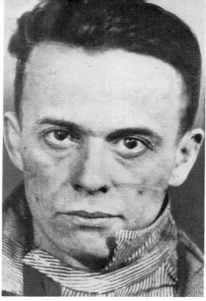

The Hamm kidnappers. (Left to right)
Byron "Monty" Bolton, Fred Barker,
Alvin Karpis.

boundaries had been violated. The death penalty was later provided in certain cases. In years to come the law was credited with having all kinds of constructive results, but the only immediate change was the emergence of the F.B.I. as a sort of a federal vigilante gang. Kidnappings continued unabated until economic conditions improved with the coming of the World War II.

A more accurate picture of the way "kidnap gangs" were organized and operated was described by Alvin "Old Creepy" Karpis, a man who achieved a certain reputation in the field.

Karpis had been a bank robber and holdup man, but the depression made money short and competition heavy. He was looking around for something to do in April 1933, when an old friend dropped in with a proposition. Why not try kidnapping? The friend, Freddie Barker, had a target picked out, and he also had a couple of professionals who needed some work: "Shotgun George" Zeigler and Monty Bolton. Both had worked for Capone and had

taken part in the St. Valentine's Day Massacre. It was not to be a syndicate operation, however. The syndicate didn't like kidnapping as a racket. It caused too much heat. They stuck to booze, whores, and gambling—products with a large degree of public acceptance.

Karpis and his pal, Barker, liked the idea. They selected two other associates, Doc Barker and Chuck Fitzgerald, and the "gang" was formed. The target was to be William Hamm, Jr., a rich brewer who lived in a big house on a hill in St. Paul, Minnesota. With 3.2 beer now legal, Hamm was making more money than he could count. He wouldn't miss a $100,000 ransom.

The "gang" rented a couple of cabins on a lake near St. Paul. From that headquarters various members checked out Hamm and made plans to grab him when he left his office at noon to walk up the hill to his home for lunch. Fitzgerald, an elderly man with an impressive appearance, was to stop Hamm and invite him over to an expensive car where

83

(Top) The home of Barthol Mey where Hamm was reportedly held captive. (Below) William W. Dunn (left) who acted as go-between for Mr. Hamm's release and (right) William Hamm, Jr., the St. Paul brewer.

Karpis, dressed as a chauffeur, would be sitting behind the wheel. Other "businessmen" were to be in the car and two others were to watch from the street in case something went wrong. As a safety precaution, the "fix" was put in with the St. Paul police headquarters should there be an effort to pull a "fast one" during the delivery of the ransom. Meanwhile, Hamm would be held in the postmaster's house in Bensenville, Illinois. The postmaster, added Karpis, was "completely trustworthy."

By June 15, everything was ready and the "snatch" went off as scheduled. Fitzgerald put on a great act and steered Hamm into the car without a moment's hesitation. Once in, the brewer was told to get down on the floor. Still Hamm wasn't aware he had been kidnapped, but he was puzzled. After a twenty-minute ride, they changed cars. Hamm was shown ransom notes and asked to sign them. He obeyed. Cotton balls were placed over his eyes and covered by dark glasses for the ride to Bensenville. The postmaster had sent his family away and was allowed to sleep on the sofa downstairs while Hamm and Karpis occupied the upstairs for five days.

Karpis developed a rather friendly feeling for his prisoner. He even worried when he had to supply him with beer made by a rival company until Hamm confessed he couldn't tell the difference when the label was removed.

The $100,000 was supposed to be dropped from one of Hamm's brewery trucks on the highway outside St. Paul. Zeigler and Freddie Barker were to pick it up. But just before the time specified for the drop, a police source tipped them the cops were going to put a machine gunner under the truck's tarpaulin to blast the pick-up men. It sounded stupid since such an action wouldn't have recovered Hamm —not alive anyway—but Karpis and his buddies had no high opinion of police intelligence. Zeigler and Barker stayed away from the scene that day, and soon sent new instructions.

Specified this time as a delivery vehicle was

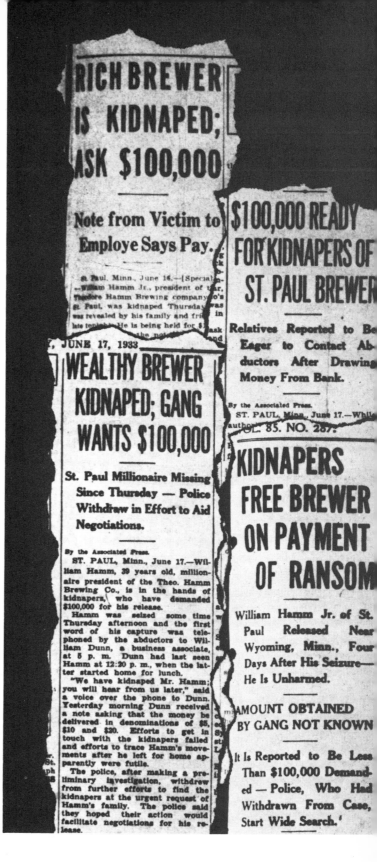

85

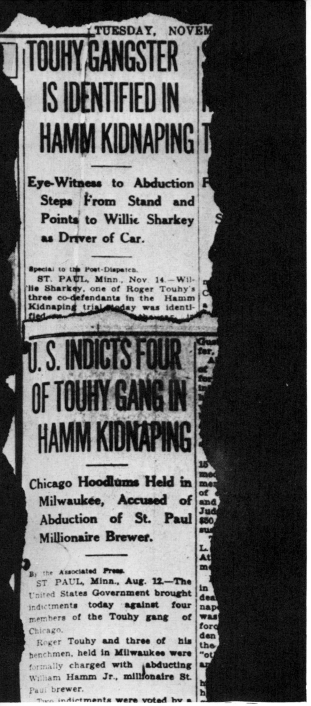

TOUHY GANGSTER IS IDENTIFIED IN HAMM KIDNAPING

Eye-Witness to Abduction Steps From Stand and Points to Willie Sharkey as Driver of Car.

Special to the Post-Dispatch.

ST. PAUL, Minn., Nov. 14.—Willie Sharkey, one of Roger Touhy's three co-defendants in the Hamm Kidnaping trial today was identified

U. S. INDICTS FOUR OF TOUHY GANG IN HAMM KIDNAPING

Chicago Hoodlums Held in Milwaukee, Accused of Abduction of St. Paul Millionaire Brewer.

By the Associated Press.

ST PAUL, Minn., Aug. 12.—The United States Government brought indictments today against four members of the Touhy gang of Chicago.

Roger Touhy and three of his henchmen, held in Milwaukee were formally charged with abducting William Hamm Jr., millionaire St. Paul brewer.

Two indictments were voted by a

(Opposite page) John Factor, known as "Jake the Barber," supposedly kidnapped by a rival gangster and released for $70,000 ransom, shown boarding a plane for Chicago. The armed guards were there to prevent gang reprisal.

a car with the side and rear doors stripped off so the driver and any passenger would be in sight all the time. The orders were followed and the pickup and getaway were clean. Zeigler and Barker walked into the postmaster's house in a happy mood. "Round up some Hamm's beer," said Zeigler, as he set down the loot-filled suitcase.

Karpis informed the prisoner that he was going home. Apparently there was no consideration given to killing Hamm and thereby eliminating the delivery problem and a potential witness. Hamm was even permitted to take a bath before departing. Karpis drove most of the night and let Hamm out in the little town of Wyoming, Minnesota. He asked his victim for ten or twenty minutes in which to get away. Hamm agreed. It was all quite civilized and almost friendly.

The kidnappers met next day in a Chicago apartment and decided to discount the money to a dealer in stolen cash. Karpis flew to Reno, Nevada, with the "hot" $100,000 and returned with a "cool" $95,000. Division was then made.

It looked like a perfect job and events later in the summer seemed to confirm that verdict. First there was the kidnapping of John Factor, known around Chicago as "Jake the Barber." At least Factor claimed he was kidnapped. The story had him leaving a roadhouse near Chicago about 11 P.M. on June 30, 1933. Allegedly, a car full of machinegunners zipped out of the darkness and forced Factor's car off the road. Factor was loaded into the kidnappers' car and it roared away into the night. Twelve days passed before Factor reappeared in a Chicago suburb. He told his tale to the police—the first they'd heard of it— and said his family had paid $70,000 to get his release.

There were cynics even then. Factor was not the most reputable of characters. His then current concern was to block his extradition to England on a $7 million stock swindle. Moreover, his son Jerome had allegedly been

Factor identifying the Touhy gang
as his kidnappers.

kidnapped a few weeks before and held for
ransom. Two pluckings of the same goose
seemed a little much. It was one of those cases
where no one really cared—except the
gangsters involved. The informed noted that
Factor had been roadhousing near the territory
of Roger "the Terrible" Touhy, the suburb of
Des Plaines. Relations were bad between
Touhy and Capone since Touhy had kept the
town off limits to Capone's vice operations.
The dispute produced a classic quote usually
attributed to Murray "the Camel" Humphreys,
who supposedly told Roger: "Al says this is
virgin territory for whorehouses." Capone was
"away" at the time of the Factor affair, but his
organization was intact and the old feud still
hot. If Jake the Barber had been kidnapped,
then the logical suspects were the Touhy gang.
But the Hamm case was the one getting the
national headlines—and the attention of the
F.B.I.

On August 12, 1933, Roger Touhy and three

companions had a bit of bad luck. They came
rolling into Elkhorn, Wisconsin, a little too
fast and wrapped their car around a telephone
pole. Police arrived, and the men explained
they were returning home from a fishing trip.
This sounded pleasant and no one was giving
anyone a hard time until one enterprising
officer decided to check out their fishing tackle.
They had plenty of it and it was good stuff
too, but they also had a rifle, some pistols, and
lots of shells. The F.B.I. office in Chicago was
notified. Shortly thereafter the special agent in
charge announced that the Touhy gang had
been arrested for kidnapping. Kidnapping
who? Why William Hamm, Jr., of course.

Touhy and his pals were duly indicted. The
nation was duly impressed. And "Old Creepy"
Karpis had a belly laugh. The heat was off.
Now he could spend that ransom money
safely.

With Melvin Purvis, the special agent in
charge of the Chicago office proclaiming, "We

88

The men Factor pointed to (left to right, seated next to table): Eddie McFadden, Albert Kaytor, Gus Schaefer and Roger Touhy. A guard is seated beside each defendant.

have an ironclad case," the Touhy gang went on trial. The jury acquitted them. The F.B.I. immediately charged them with kidnapping Jake the Barber. Hell, they were just hoods, after all. Rats. Purvis was back with a statement. "This case," he said, referring to the Factor kidnapping, "holds a particular interest for me because it represents a triumph of deductive detective work. We assumed from the start, with no material evidence, that the Touhy gang was responsible for the crime."

A lot of people remained unconvinced that a crime had been committed. Touhy charged that it was a frame—an example of the F.B.I. pulling the Capone syndicate's chestnuts from the fire in order to cover up its own goof. The first trial ended in a hung jury, but the second time around Roger the Terrible was convicted and sentenced to ninety-nine years in prison. As he was led away from the courtroom he vomited.

Factor came out ahead. In order to keep

him around to testify, his extradition to England was stopped. He never did stand trial although he reportedly paid back about 20 per cent of the sum swindled.

Touhy broke out of prison in 1942 and enjoyed a few weeks of liberty before the F.B.I. captured him. The agency had a federal handle on him with the charge that Touhy was a draft dodger. He went back to prison with an additional 199 years tacked on to his sentence.

Some years later a hearing for Touhy was secured before Judge John H. Barnes. It lasted thirty-six days, and at the end the judge ruled:

"The court finds that John Factor was not kidnapped for ransom or otherwise on the night of June 30th or July 1, 1933, though he was taken as a result of his own connivance . . . The court finds that Roger Touhy did not kidnap John Factor . . ."

It was five years later, however, before Touhy was freed, for the state appealed the

SAYS HE GUARDED URSCHEL 4 DAYS UNDER THREATS

R. G. Shannon Testifies George Kelly and Albert Bates Took Blindfolded Man to His Texas Farm.

HE GOT CHECK FOR $1500 AFTERWARD

Declares Step - Daughter, Kelly's Wife, Sent It — Taken to Oklahoma With Wife and Son for Trial.

By the Associated Press.

OKLAHOMA CITY, Ok., Aug. 25.—An airplane bearing Mr. and Mrs. R. G. Shannon and their son, Armon, from Fort Worth in custody of Federal officers arrived here this afternoon. Several carloads of heavily armed officers met the plane and escorted the prisoners to the county jail.

By the Associated Press.

FORT WORTH, Tex., Aug. 25 G. (B___non,

(Top right) Charles F. Urschel and (bottom right) W. R. Jarrett, the kidnapped oilmen.

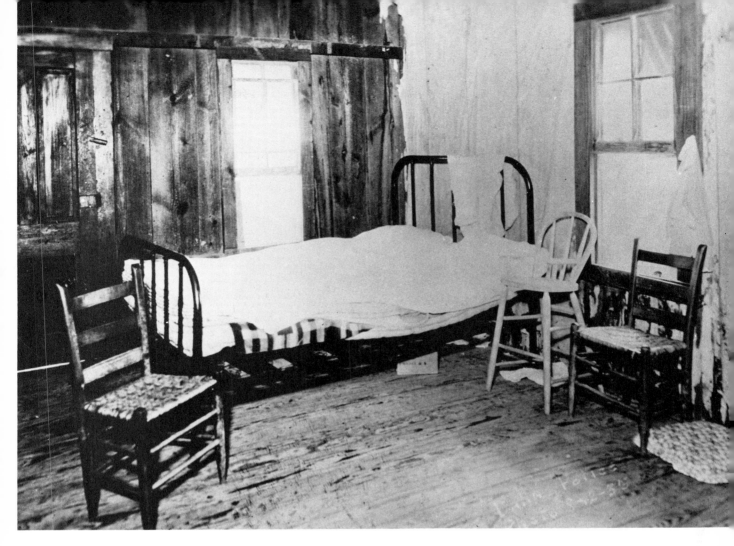

(Left) Armon Shannon's home near Paradise, Texas, where Urschel was held for ransom in 1923.
(Above) The interior of the shack where Charles F. Urschel stayed during his captivity.

(Top) This twelve-year-old from
Memphis, Tennessee, Geraldine Arnold,
was responsible for the arrest of
"Machine Gun" Kelly and his wife.
She also gave testimony which resulted
in the conviction of the two people
who harbored them.
(Below) The Urschel trial was the first
time that sound motion picture
equipment was allowed in a
federal courtroom.

judge's decision. Finally, to end the legal logjam, the governor of Illinois commuted Touhy's sentence to seventy-two years and he was released on parole in November 1959. Twenty-three days later, on December 16, he was blasted by two shotguns and died within the hour. His killers were never found.

A few months after Touhy was murdered, ex-special agent in charge, Melvin Purvis, killed himself.

But an organization as dedicated and as publicized as the F.B.I. wins more than it loses. At the very time the Factor-Hamm kidnappings were being bungled, the FBI was achieving its greatest coup of the period—the solution of the Urschel kidnapping.

It began on the night of July 22, 1933. Oil man Charles F. Urschel and his recent bride, Berenice, were playing bridge with their neighbors on the porch of their beautiful home in Oklahoma City, Oklahoma. Suddenly the screen door opened and two men with guns walked in. They wanted Urschel, they said, and since neither Urschel nor his neighbor, Walter Jarrett, spoke, they took both men.

The women called the police and the F.B.I. Urschel was a rich oil man and his wife, the widow of Tom Slick, another oil millionaire, was wealthy in her own right. Moreover Urschel was a personal friend of the nation's new president, a fact not likely to be overlooked by F.B.I. Director John Edgar Hoover. Indeed, President Roosevelt was to take a personal interest in the case.

Police and the local F.B.I. representative rushed to the house. About ninety minutes later Jarrett came back. He had been dropped some nine miles from town after the bandits finally got Urschel's identification straight. He had bummed a ride home.

The press arrived. The story made bold headlines across the country and citizens everywhere began to enjoy the live soap opera. While it was deadly serious for the Urschels and their friends, as well as for the kidnappers, for almost everyone else it was melodrama in daily installments.

On July 26, four days after the kidnapping, the ransom note arrived. It demanded "TWO HUNDRED THOUSAND DOLLARS ($200,000) in GENUINE USED FEDERAL RESERVE CURRENCY in the denominations of TWENTY DOLLAR ($20.00) bills." Willingness to pay was to be signaled by running the following ad for one week in the *Daily Oklahoman:*

FOR SALE—160 acres land, good five-room house, deep well. Also cows, tools, tractors, corn and hay. $3,750.00 for quick sale TERMS. Box No. ___.

If it sounds like a bargain today, the price was common enough in that time of economic catastrophe and not likely to attract attention. The ad was quickly placed; Box 807 was assigned. Two days later it drew a response, an air mail letter postmarked in Joplin, Missouri. The family was instructed to send the money by E.E. Fitzgerald, a friend of Urschel. The plan was a variation of the train ride taken in 1874 by the father of Charlie Ross, and it was to prove just as futile. The train was to go to Kansas City. Somewhere along the way, the note instructed, a fire would be seen burning on the right side of the track. Shortly after that would be another fire and it was there that the money in a light-colored suitcase should be thrown on the track.

Fitzgerald and a friend made the long trip standing on the vestibule of a Pullman. But no lights burned along the way and when daylight came they were in Kansas City. The note had provided for failure. In the event of the "slightest hitch," Fitzgerald was to go to the Muehlebach Hotel in Kansas City, register as E.E. Kincaid, and await instructions. He obeyed, still lugging the bag containing $200,000. At 10 A.M. a telegram arrived for

One of the letters that Urschel wrote while kidnapped.

Herbert K. Hyde, Chief Prosecutor,
holding the chains found in the
Shannon home where Harvey J. Bailey
and several other accomplices of
"Machine Gun" Kelly were captured.
Urschel had been bound with
the chains.

Kincaid. It promised to communicate about
6 P.M.

The call came at 5:45 P.M. Fitzgerald was
told to take a cab to the La Salle Hotel and
then to start walking west. With the money, of
course. His friend could not accompany him.

This time no hitch developed. Fitzgerald
spotted two cars parked on the street ahead
and assumed he was under the guns of the
men they contained. Down the street toward
him walked a tall man, husky, but "stylishly
dressed in a natty summer suit with a turned
down Panama hat. He wore two-tone shoes;
his tie was immaculately knotted into the
collar of his well-fitting two-toned shirt." Yet
his glance was "furtive."

The stranger stopped. "I'll take that grip,"
he said.

Fitzgerald permitted him to do so but only
after receiving assurance that Urschel would be
home within twelve hours.

The time allotted passed and still Urschel
did not appear. Twenty-four hours went by.
The family waited. At about 9 P.M. on the
night after the payment was made, he walked
up to his house, but the F.B.I. agent on duty
wouldn't let him in until a friend of the family
had identified him as the central actor in the
far-ranging drama.

Within ten minutes of Urschel's return,
F.B.I. brass was in his home to ask questions.
The oil man pleaded fatigue but talked for
thirty minutes before his bride demanded he be
allowed to rest. The session resumed next
morning and lasted for eight hours without
interruption. The F.B.I. knew a good witness
when it saw one.

Urschel was a good witness because he was
a disciplined man who noticed everything and
filed it away for later reference. His
recollection of events was a mosaic of
individual bits of information. By themselves
they meant nothing, but collectively they
provided the clues that broke the case quickly.

He described the long ride over dirt roads,
the roosters he heard signaling dawn, a change

(Standing, left to right) Albert Bates,
Harvey Bailey, Armon Shannon,
R. G. Shannon, and Mrs. Shannon.
All but Armon Shannon, the son, were
convicted and given life sentences in
Oklahoma City, Oklahoma, for the
kidnapping of Charles Urschel.
Armon was given a ten-year
suspended sentence.

of cars in a barnyard somewhere, and finally
stopping at a house. When morning came he
ate a "meager breakfast" while blindfolded.
Someone read to him the headlines from the
newspaper which concerned the kidnapping.
That evening he was moved about a mile away
to another house where he was handcuffed to a
baby's high chair and slept on a quilt on the
floor. He then wrote letters as his captors
required to his wife and friends.

Urschel continued with minute descriptions
of everything: the day-by-day events, the
weather, the conversation, the interior of the
shack, the appearance of those captors he saw.
All this detail proved valuable later, but most
important of all was his recollection that an
airplane had passed above the house each day
at 9:45 A.M. and 5:45 P.M. except on Sunday
morning, July 30.

He had pinpointed the time by counting off
the seconds after the plane passed until several
minutes had elapsed. Then he would

innocently inquire as to the time. By
subtracting the minutes he had counted from
the time given, he estimated the exact moment
the plane passed. It was something to do, an
intellectual exercise, and he had a hunch it
might be useful information.

It was.

He also remembered being given water in a
handleless tin cup. The water had a mineral
taste and it came from a well on the northwest
side of the house. When the bucket was drawn
up, the windlass creaked.

There were other clues. He recalled, for
instance, that during the long drive on the
night he was kidnapped, they had encountered
a hard shower of rain and the car almost got
stuck. Then later they stopped for gas and he
heard the woman who sold it remark that the
rain wouldn't help the crops but might help
the broom corn. There was more rain that
night when they reached the hideout. A week
later, on Sunday—the day he didn't hear the

95

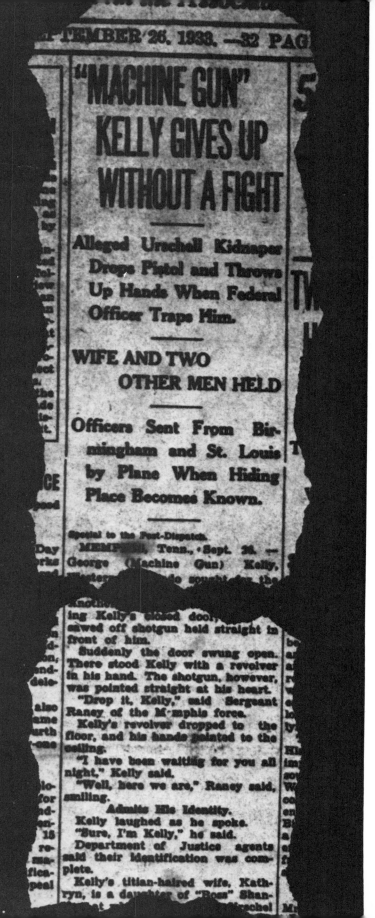

SEPTEMBER 26, 1933.—32 PAGES

"MACHINE GUN" KELLY GIVES UP WITHOUT A FIGHT

Alleged Urschel Kidnaper Drops Pistol and Throws Up Hands When Federal Officer Traps Him.

WIFE AND TWO OTHER MEN HELD

Officers Sent From Birmingham and St. Louis by Plane When Hiding Place Becomes Known.

Special to the Post-Dispatch.

MEMPHIS, Tenn., Sept. 26.— George (Machine Gun) Kelly, ...

... ing Kelly's closed door, sawed off shotgun held straight in front of him.

Suddenly the door swung open. There stood Kelly with a revolver in his hand. The shotgun, however, was pointed straight at his heart.

"Drop it, Kelly," said Sergeant Raney of the Memphis force.

Kelly's revolver dropped to the floor, and his hands pointed to the ceiling.

"I have been waiting for you all night," Kelly said.

"Well, here we are," Raney said, smiling.

Admits His Identity.

Kelly laughed as he spoke.

"Sure, I'm Kelly," he said.

Department of Justice agents said their identification was complete.

Kelly's titian-haired wife, Kathryn, is a daughter of "Boss" Shan...

plane in the morning—there was a hard, driving rain.

The F.B.I. checked weather reports and airplane schedules. Soon they pinpointed the little community of Paradise, Texas. It fit all the clues Urschel offered. Indeed, it was found that the American Airlines pilot on his regular run had dodged Paradise that Sunday morning to miss a thunderstorm.

A team of agents went to Paradise and began visiting farms in the guise of bankers seeking to extend loans to farmers. Eventually one came to the five hundred-acre "ranch" of R.G. Shannon and instantly knew he had found his prize. Every detail of the house and yard fit the description given by Urschel. The agent wiped his brow and asked for a drink of water from the well. The water had a strong mineral taste.

As quickly as the agent, Edward Dowd, reported his finding, the pieces began to fall into place. Shannon's step-daughter was the wife of George "Machine Gun" Kelly, one of the F.B.I.'s "most wanted" men. A bank robber of considerable experience, Kelly had a local reputation. That reputation was to be considerably inflated in the months to come.

A squad of F.B.I. agents and hand-picked police officers was assembled. Urschel went along for the ride. The raiders struck at dawn and found everyone at the Shannon farm asleep. Shannon was arrested first. Then, asleep on a cot, Harvey Bailey was found, a giant of a man who was much wanted in connection with the Union Station Massacre at Kansas City a few months before. He was considered a great prize.

Others at the farm were women, one of them the daughter of Katherine Kelly, wife of the outlaw, by another marriage. One room of the shack was filled with expensive clothing for men and women—obviously it was the Kellys' bedroom, but the Kellys were not there. The barn on the farm contained a mountain of bailed hay in which had been fashioned a hiding place where a man could lie and watch

(Opposite page) A news clipping
which quotes what ''Machine Gun''
Kelly actually said during his capture.
(Above) Three acquitted during the
Urschel kidnap trial (left to right):
Sam Kronick, Isidore Blumenfield
and Sam Kosberg.

the house and road. It was empty, luckily, but there was evidence it had been occupied until recently.

Urschel enjoyed the proceedings as he revisited places and things he had earlier described. Bailey was searched and seven hundred dollars of the ransom money was found in his pockets. But greater thrills were to come. The raid was extended to the home of Shannon's son, Armon. It was a mile away and out of sight. Again surprise was achieved, but no one was at home except for Armon and his young wife, Oletha. While the agents talked to the frightened couple, Urschel explored the shack and yard. Everything was as he had described it—even the baby's high chair to which he had been handcuffed.

Young Shannon decided to cooperate. He talked. His father soon followed suit, and, after some delay, Mrs. Shannon joined the chorus. Implicated were several hoodlums, the most important of whom was Machine Gun Kelly. Second in interest was Albert Bates, who was also missing when the farm was raided. He was captured by Denver police on August 14. On August 23 a federal grand jury indicted Bates, Bailey, and eleven others for the kidnapping of Charles F. Urschel.

Among those named were Isadore Blumenfeld of Minneapolis, and several of his associates. They were charged with dealing in "hot" money—the $200,000 ransom—and with changing part of it into cash the Kellys could pass. Blumenfeld was better known as "Kid Cann," and his outfit as "the Minneapolis Combination," an important part of organized crime.

It is perhaps unnecessary to add that on September 30, 1933, the indictment against Blumenfeld was squashed. Two of his men, Ed Berman and Clifford Skelly, took the rap for the boss and went to prison for five years. Blumenfeld and his brother, the infamous Yiddy Bloom, went on to become millionaires many times over. They invested heavily in Florida real estate in conjunction with Meyer

"MACHINE GUN AND WIFE GE KIDNAPPING

George "Machine Gun" Kelly and his wife are sentenced for their part in the Charles F. Urschel kidnapping. (Right) Letter to Urschel from Kelly, with his fingerprints at the bottom.

I guarant charles,
Just a few lines
let you know that I
are going my plans
laid to destroy your
so called Mansion, and
you and your family
immediately after their
And you fellow
will be g

will be out for the
ceremonies, "your clanging"
Now Sap - it is
up to you, if the
thomans are convited
you can get your and
rich wife in Hell, because
that will be the only
place you can use one.
"Adios" smart one
"your worst enemy.
Geo. R. Kelly.
I will put my print
below so you can't say
some crank wrot this.
(over)

Kidnaped Banker, Home and Wife

RESIDENCE in St. Paul, Minn., of EDWARD BREMER, of the Commercial State Bank and member of wealthy family, who is being held for $200,000 ransom. Portraits are those of missing man and MRS. BREMER.

TWO WOMEN HELD ON GRAFT

...OWA INQUIRY

...rokerage' They

...der-
...men
...raft
...an

$200,000 READY FOR BANKER'S KIDNAPERS

St. Paul Brewer Pleads for Return of Son—No Contact With Abductors.

By the Associated Press.
ST. PAUL, Minn., Jan. 2?. — A fortune in old bills was ready for kidnapers...if they would...

Lansky, and despite long "rap sheets" become accepted as responsible "businessmen" in the Florida community.

The case illustrates how in the thirties the "punks" got the headlines and the punishment, while syndicate personalities were quietly building empires that would endure for decades and become accepted as part of the economic and social structure of the nation.

The Kellys were still being hunted on September 18, 1933, when the trial of Bates, Bailey, and the Shannons began; Justice was swifter then. On the same day Kelly wrote a letter to his kidnap victim. Addressed to "Ignorant Charles," it said in part:

Just a few lines to let you know I am getting my plans made to destroy your so-called mansion, and you and your family immediately after this trial . . . I am spending your money to have you and your family killed—nice—eh? You are bucking people who have cash—planes, bombs, and unlimited connections both here and abroad. . . . If my brain was no larger than yours, the Government would have had me long ago. As it is I am drinking good beer and will yet see you and your family like I should have left you at first—stone dead.

Now say—it is up to you; if the Shannons are convicted, you can get another rich wife in hell, because that will be the only place you can use one.

Kelly added a postscript: he was placing his fingerprint on the letter, he said, "so you can't say some crank wrote this." And he did.

The day after receiving the letter, Urschel testified for hours about his experience. If he was shaken by Kelly's threats, no one reported it.

The trial was still going on when on the morning of September 26, the jurors in the courtroom heard a newsboy on the street shout:

"Extra! Extra! Machine Gun Kelly captured."

The Kellys had moved around the country like gypsies before coming to earth in Memphis. The F.B.I. was right behind them. On that morning of September 26, Memphis

Katherine Kelly with her husband in
chains behind her, as they are led
into the courthouse for trial.

police and F.B.I. agents broke down the front
door of the house in which the couple was
hiding. Kelly, still in bed when the crash
sounded, opened his bedroom door and looked
out to see what was causing the commotion.
Detective Sergeant W.J. Raney, who along
with Detectives A.O. Clark and Floyd
Wiebenga had broken through the door, stuck
a shotgun barrel into Kelly's stomach and
ordered him to drop his gun. Kelly obeyed,
letting his automatic fall to the floor.

Around this incident a legend has arisen.
Writers who got their information only from
the F.B.I. have pictured Kelly cringing before
the officers and pleading, "Don't shoot,
G-Men!" Allegedly, this was the first time the
F.B.I. had been called that—short for
government men—and it stuck.

In reality, the term "G-Men" had been used
before in reference to employees of the federal
government. The Memphis officers who made
the arrest have stated again and again that
Kelly said nothing about "G-Men." Yet the

legend has persisted, thanks to constant
repetition by writers friendly to the then
director of the F.B.I., Hoover. Why the F.B.I.
which had done a wonderful job of translating
Urschel's recollections into evidence should
cap such an achievement with this shoddy bit
of image-building is hard to comprehend. But
Hoover had almost been fired when Roosevelt
took office, and he apparently was determined
to achieve political security by public relations
methods. Aiding, of course, was the press
which would quote and requote any official
whose statements were colorful enough.

On September 30, the jury found all the
original defendants guilty: the Shannons,
Bailey, Bates, and the two Minneapolis
money-changers who took the blame to protect
their boss. Before sentence was passed,
Katherine and George Kelly were arraigned.
The government expected them to plead guilty
and wanted the judge to sentence everyone at
the same time and thus wrap up the case.
Unexpectedly, the Kellys refused to cooperate.

Another trial was going to be necessary after all.

It didn't take long. On October 12, 1933, the jury found the Kellys guilty and the judge sentenced them to life imprisonment. Katherine was heard to mutter: "My Pekinese dog would have gotten a life sentence in this court." Outside the building, disillusioned newsboys watched Kelly come out and they began to shout: "Read all about Pop-gun Kelly." The trial, among other things, had shown Kelly's fearsome reputation was largely a myth. But, as the reporters say, it had been a good story while it lasted.

The F.B.I. kept up the act. Eight agents armed with machine guns guarded Kelly on the train to Leavenworth. A year later he was sent to Alcatraz upon its completion. From that grim prison he wrote a long and surprisingly literate letter to Urschel on April 11, 1940. After asking about possible oil strikes on his farm in Wise County, Texas, he added:

Now before I go further don't think I am merely writing this letter to try to get into your good graces. You can rest assured I will never ask you to do anything toward getting me out. Naturally, I realize that your enmity could become a detriment in later years. So, to be truthful, I hope you do not feel too vindictive; although I hardly think that you are a person of a malevolent disposition. After so many years, I must admit that I am rather ashamed of the grandstand play that I made in the courtroom. I was good and mad at the time. Need I remind you of the enthusiasm of the days during my trial? You and your friends shared in it; seemed to revel in it. What produced it? The Department of Justice's love of the dramatic? The public's desire for a good free show? An accumulated spirited vitality which found no employment in the things of the day and so was ready to enjoy to the utmost anything out of the ordinary?

Kelly ended the long letter by revealing the "secret of how to do easy time." You just let things "drift along." But then he added:

(Above, right) Edward G. Bremer, who spent 22 days in the hands of kidnappers who collected $200,000 for his release. Bremer is shown here with his father.
(Right) The house in Bensenville, Illinois, where he was held captive.

I must be fair. Being in prison has brought me one positive advantage. It could hardly do less. It's name is comradeship—a rough kindness of man to man; unselfishness; an absence, or a diminution, of the tendency to look ahead, at least very far ahead; a carelessness, though it is bred of despair; a clinging to life and the possible happiness it may offer at some future date . . .

But for Kelly there was no escape. He was returned to Leavenworth Penitentiary in 1951. The climate on Alcatraz had always bothered him. In 1954 he suffered a heart attack and died. His wife was more fortunate; her case was reopened in 1958. Her attorney argued that her trial had been unfair. The federal judge ordered the F.B.I. to produce its records. The F.B.I. refused. The judge then set aside the conviction. His ruling was later reversed, and the case was sent back for a continuation of the hearing. The F.B.I. still refused to produce its records and the hearing never resumed. Katherine and her mother remained free after twenty-five years in prison.

Before leaving the thirties with its quick "justice," its uncomplicated good guys vs. bad guys drama, and its hysterical reporting, we should, perhaps, complete the saga of "Old Creepy" Karpis.

The kidnapping of William Hamm, Jr., had gone so well, some of the boys wanted to pull another "snatch." And they had a subject— Edward Bremer, president of the Commercial Bank of St. Paul. Karpis has since maintained that he didn't think much of the idea— Bremer's father was close to President Roosevelt and that meant federal heat—but he allowed himself to be persuaded. It seemed logical that, with reaction setting in, the best days for free-lance free enterprise were about over. Before long one would have to quit or join the syndicate. The temptation to make one last big "score" was too great to resist.

January 19, 1934, was the day. Bremer's car was blocked after he had dropped his daughter

IDENTIFICATION ORDER NO. 1218
March 22, 1934.

DIVISION OF INVESTIGATION
U. S. DEPARTMENT OF JUSTICE
WASHINGTON, D. C.

Fingerprint Classification

13 1 8r 5
─────
1 U 7

WANTED

ALVIN KARPIS, with aliases,
A. CARTER, RAYMOND HADLEY, GEORGE HALLER, ALVIN KORPIS,
EARL PEEL, GEORGE DUNN, R. E. HAMILTON, RAY HUNTER.

KIDNAPING

DESCRIPTION

Age, 25 years (1934); Height, 5 feet,
9-3/4 inches; weight, 130 pounds;
Build, slender; hair, brown; Eyes,
blue; Complexion, fair;
Marks, 1 inch cut scar lower knuckle
left index finger.

RELATIVES:

Mr. John Karpis, father, 2842 North
Francisco Avenue, Chicago, Illinois.
Mrs. Anna Karpis, mother, 2842 North
Francisco Avenue, Chicago, Illinois.
Mrs. Emily Newbold, sister, 2840 North
Francisco Avenue, Chicago, Illinois.
Mrs. Robert (Clara) Venuto, sister,
1829 West Erie Street, Chicago,
Illinois.
Mrs. Albert (Amelia) Grooms, sister,
1234 North Monroe Street,
Topeka, Kansas.

Photograph taken May 19, 1930.

K-716

Alvin Karpis

CRIMINAL RECORD

As Alvin Karpis, #7071, received State
Industrial Reformatory, Hutchinson, Kansas,
February 25, 1926; crime, burglary-2nd
degree; sentence, 10 years; escaped March
9, 1929; returned March 25, 1930.

As Raymond Hadley, #17902, arrested
Police Department, Kansas City, Missouri,
March 23, 1930; charge, larceny-auto and
safe blower; released to State Industrial
Reformatory, Hutchinson, Kansas, as an
escape.

As Alvin Karpis, #1535, received State
Penitentiary, Lansing, Kansas, May 19, 1930 –
transferred from State Industrial Reformatory;
crime, burglary-2nd degree; sentence, 5 to 10
years.

As George Haller, #8008, arrested Police
Department, Tulsa, Oklahoma, June 10, 1931;
charge, investigation-burglary; delivered
Police Department, Okmulgee, Oklahoma.

As A. Korpis, #1609, arrested Police Department, Okmulgee, Oklahoma, June 10, 1931; charge, burglary;
sentenced September 11, 1931, 4 years, State Penitentiary, McAlester, Oklahoma; paroled.

Alvin Karpis is wanted for questioning in connection with the kidnaping of Edward G. Bremer at St. Paul, Minnesota, on
January 17, 1934.

Law enforcement agencies kindly transmit any additional information or criminal record to the nearest office of the Division
of Investigation, U. S. Department of Justice.

If apprehended, please notify the Director, Division of Investigation, U. S. Department of Justice, Washington, D. C., or
the Special Agent in Charge of the office of the Division of Investigation listed on the back hereof which is nearest your city.

(over)

Issued by: J. EDGAR HOOVER, DIRECTOR.

at a private school. Two men jumped in beside Bremer, intending to shuffle him to the rear seat while driving off his car. Bremer resisted, however, and it was necessary for Doc Barker to slug him over the head.

At a rendezvous outside of town, Bremer was told to sign three ransom notes addressed to his father. He was still bleeding and gave trouble. He continued to give trouble after they got him safely to their hideout in Bensenville. Bremer's father gave trouble as well, and the negotiations dragged on and on. Meanwhile, Roosevelt had personally ordered the F.B.I. into action and the entire area swarmed with "feds." Even some vacationing hoods down in Owney's Madden's new capital, Hot Springs, Arkansas, were pulled out of the hot baths where they were treating their syphilis, and were questioned.

It was twenty days after the kidnapping before Shotgun George Zeigler and Freddie Barker came staggering in under the weight of $200,000 in marked bills. Gratefully, Karpis burned all of Bremer's old clothing, dressed him in a new outfit, and took him to Rochester, Minnesota. Bremer complained all the way about his old garters, Karpis said. They were the best garters he'd ever owned and Karpis had burned them. With a sense of relief "Old Creepy" told his prisoner to "beat it" in Rochester.

The F.B.I. soon announced that the kidnapping had been the work of the Karpis-Barker Gang. Fingerprints left on abandoned gasoline cans and an unusual flashlight dropped near the scene of the kidnapping were the clues. Karpis kept moving about the country. He had his big score, but when the loot was divided it came to only $25,000 per man. And even that was so "hot" the Reno money-changers refused to touch it.

Ultimately, Karpis' friends were picked off one by one. In the process, "Ma Barker," mother of Freddie and Doc Barker, was killed. The F.B.I., with help from the press, immediately turned her into "Bloody Mama,"

(Opposite page) Alvin "Creepy" Karpis' arrest record.
(Above) J. Edgar Hoover, director of the Federal Bureau of Investigation.

the "brains" of the Karpis-Barker Gang. It was absurd and no evidence was produced to support it, but like the "G-Man" quote attributed to Machine Gun Kelly, it became part of the mythology of the day and lives on.

Karpis was captured on May 1, 1936, in New Orleans. Director Hoover was present to take a bow and build the G-Man legend. His presence also made possible a revealing bit of dialogue.

For some reason shortly after the capture, Hoover referred to his prize as a "hoodlum."

"I'm no hoodlum," said Karpis. "I'm a thief."

Hoover didn't know the difference. Karpis tried to explain:

"A thief," he said, "is anybody who gets out and works for his living, like robbing a bank or breaking into a place and stealing stuff, or kidnapping somebody. He really gives some effort to it. A hoodlum is a pretty lousy kind of scum. He works for gangsters and bumps off guys after they've been put on the spot. Why, after I'd made my rep, some of the Chicago Syndicate wanted me to go to work for them as a hood—you know, handling a machine gun. They offered me two hundred and fifty dollars a week and all the protection I needed. I was on the lam at the time and not able to work at my regular line. But I wouldn't consider it. 'I'm a thief,' I said. 'I'm no lousy hoodlum.' "

"From my standpoint," said Hoover, "you're still a hoodlum."

A quarter-century would pass before Hoover acknowledged that organized crime existed.

Meanwhile Karpis decided to plead guilty and avoid a Kelly-type circus. He was sentenced to life imprisonment on one count involving the Hamm kidnapping. In 1969 he was paroled and deported to his native Canada where in 1971 he wrote *The Alvin Karpis Story*.

5. AN EYE FOR AN EYE

One leaves the black and white days of the 1930's with some regret. Things were simpler then—or seemed to be to a lot of people.

When on November 9, 1933, in San Jose, California, Thomas Thurmond and John Holmes kidnapped and murdered twenty-two-year-old Brooke Hart, heir to a department-store fortune, both police and citizens saw no need to wait for the F.B.I. Thurmond was arrested while still on the telephone to Alex Hart, the father, giving instructions as to how the $40,000 in ransom was to be delivered. After some persuasion he implicated Holmes who was just as quickly picked up. The two were jailed in downtown San Jose. Nine days later their victim's body washed ashore. A crowd estimated at 15,000 people collected quickly. Sheriff William Emig called Governor James "Sunny Jim" Rolfe and asked for troops. Rolfe refused. Within an hour the mob assaulted the jail. Local and state police battled for an hour, using pressure hoses and tear-gas, but in vain. Ultimately the door was battered down and the two prisoners taken out and hanged from trees in the

adjoining park. Governor Rolfe applauded. The Lynch mob, he said, supplied "the best lesson ever given the country. I would like to parole all kidnappers in San Quentin and Folsom to the fine, patriotic citizens of San Jose."

In the 1930's another Charlie Ross was kidnapped. In this instance, however, the Ross was a seventy-two-year-old greeting card manufacturer of Chicago. On the night of September 25, 1937, Ross and his secretary were forced off the road by two men who intended only to rob them. When the robbers approached the stalled car with drawn guns, however, Ross assumed it was a kidnapping and said so. From that moment on, it was.

The "brains" of the operation was John Henry Seadlund, a small-time burglar and tramp. He shared one passion with F.B.I. Director Hoover, however—a love of the horses. Ultimately that was to be Seadlund's downfall.

The ransom of $50,000 was collected but Charles S. Ross was not returned. By some good detective work, the F.B.I. discovered

An enraged mob batters down the
door of the San Jose, California, jail
to remove John M. Holmes and Thomas
H. Thurmond, confessed kidnap
slayers of Brooke Hart. A cloud of
tear gas is visible in the background.
The mob ripped off the two men's
clothes and strung the prisoners
up on trees in a park opposite the jail.

(Opposite page) The epitaph to the
kidnappers of Brooke Hart.

ST-DISPATCH FINAL

lue With the Associated Press News Service

NOVEMBER 27, 1933.—30 PAGES

BLUE SEAL

PRICE CEN

KIDNAPERS OF HART TAKEN FROM JAIL, LYNCHED BY MOB

LYNCHING 'A FINE LESSON TO WHOLE NATION,' SAYS GOV. ROLPH OF CALIFORNIA

By the Associated Press.

SACRAMENTO, Nov. 27.—Gov. JAMES ROLPH JR. said today the lynching in San Jose last night of Thomas Thurmond and John Holmes, confessed kidnapers and slayers of Brooke Hart, should result in fewer kidnapings throughout the country and that he would pardon any one arrested for the lynchings.

"That was a fine lesson to the whole nation," Gov. Rolph said. "There will be less kidnaping in the country now. They made a good job of it.

"If anyone is arrested for the good job, I'll pardon them all. I hope this lesson will serve in every state of the Union."

The Governor postponed his trip to Boise, Idaho, to attend a Governors' conference, not for the purpose of being on hand to call out troops but to prevent it.

"If I had gone away someone would have called out the troops," the Governor said, "and I promised in Los Angeles I would not do that. Why should I call out troops to protect those two fellows?

"The people make the laws, don't they?" he asked. "Well, if the people have confidence that troops will not be called out to mow them down when they seek to protect themselves against kidnapers . . . liable . . .

Lynched Kidnapers, Man They Killed

M. HOLMES,
THUR-
HART.

THOUSANDS CHEER AS MURDERERS ARE HANGED

San Jose Police and Deputies Fight Crowd of 100 for Two Hours Before Doors of Lock Up Are Battered Down.

KILLERS STRUNG UP IN MID-TOWN PARK

Officers Use Tear Gas in Futile Attempt to Rout Raiders—Hart's Body Recovered a Few Hours Earlier.

By the Associated Press.

SAN JOSE, Cal., Nov. 27. — Thomas H. Thurmond and John M. Holmes, confessed kidnaper-murderers of Brooke L. Hart, lynched here last night by a . . . who . . .

109

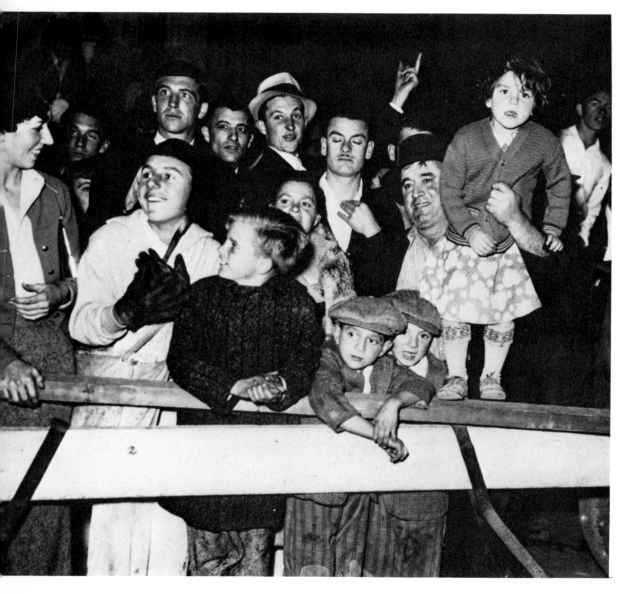

(Opposite page) As if they were at a
circus, 6,000 spectators, women and
children among them, witnessed the
lynching of the two prisoners.
Hanging (above) is the body of
Thomas Thurmond. Governor Rolfe of
California said he would pardon any
lynchers arrested.

Seadlund's identity and his love of horses. When the marked bills of the ransom money began turning up in cities having race tracks, it was possible to anticipate Seadlund's movements. The trail pointed toward Santa Anita. F.B.I. agents were placed in every betting window to check all bets. On January 14, 1938, Seadlund appeared at the $10 window. Arrested, he admitted his guilt and took the agents to a spot in Spooner, Wisconsin, where he had buried Ross and his own erstwhile partner, James Gray. The agents dug up the body. More surprising, they recovered $47,345 of the ransom. It seems that Seadlund really knew horses and had won as much as he lost. All he had needed was a bankroll to begin.

Some two months after his arrest, he died in the Cook County electric chair. Not even the folks in San Jose could have done it much quicker than that.

If space permitted it might be instructive to examine certain other cases of the period: the Alice Speed Stoll kidnapping in Louisville; the George Weyerhaeuser episode in Tacoma; and the James Cash affair in Miami. But, for the most part, these and other cases followed the pattern of the times.

The rash of kidnapping tapered off eventually. While the F.B.I. and capital punishment took most of the credit, the real reason seemed to be the return of prosperity with the approach of World War II. The 1940's were relatively free of kidnapping. Money was plentiful and there was employment for everyone—in the army and out. Additionally, the 1930's sense of betrayal had been swept aside in an outburst of patriotism. The Japanese attack on Pearl Harbor in 1941 brought the people and their government together again in a common unity of purpose. True, the crime syndicates played the black market and did some war profiteering on a large scale, but the enterprising individual and the free-lance gang became memories. Even in the 1950's during

3 GUNMEN KIDNAP RICH AUTOIST ON LONELY HIGHWAY

Woman Guest Tells of Abduction Mystery

Silence Hides Victim's Fate as Hours Pass

Charles S. Ross, wealthy retired greeting card manufacturer, still was missing early today, more than two days since his kidnaping Saturday in Wolf road, southwest of Franklin Park. Investigators admitted they were no nearer a solution of the crime than they were when it was first reported.

No demand for ransom had been made, but Mrs. Ross, in her apartment at 2932 Commonwealth avenue, was waiting patiently in the hope that some word would be received from him or his captors.

Mrs. Charles S. Ross.

One witness, whose information was regarded as important in view of the general absence of clews, came to Chicago from Sycamore yesterday, but returned before he was interviewed by Capt. Daniel Gilbert of the state's attorney's office.

Bellboy Tells of Meeting.

He is Cecil Vandiver, 19 years old, who has been a bellboy in the hotel at S——

112

In the north woods near Spooner,
Wisconsin, federal agents found the
bodies of Charles S. Ross and
James Atwood Gray.

A photograph taken by John Henry
Seadlund, the kidnapper of Charles S.
Ross, who was holding a newspaper
in his hand to date the fact that he
was still alive.

the trauma of the McCarthy Era and the various "Eisenhower Recessions," there was no epidemic of kidnapping comparable to that of the 1930's. The F.B.I. had consolidated its position, first as "spy chasers" during the war and later as "Red hunters," and no longer needed to shoot down bank robbers or to exaggerate the evil of kidnappers. And with no one to quote on the subject, the press accepted as gospel the notion that, with a few exceptions, kidnapping was a thing of the past.

A major exception was the September 28, 1953, kidnapping of Bobby Greenlease, Jr., whose father owned a Cadillac dealership in Kansas City, Missouri.

The actual kidnapping followed the technique developed in the 1909 snatch of Willie Whitla. Six-year-old Bobby was taken from school on the pretext that his mother was ill and wanted him immediately. Sister Morand at Bobby's exclusive school didn't hesitate when a nervous, middle-aged woman made the request that Bobby accompany her.

A cab was waiting and the woman and the boy got in and rode downtown. At 40th and Main Streets, the two passengers alighted and got into a station wagon driven by a ruddy-faced man. It drove away immediately.

Meanwhile, back at the school, a sister called the hospital to inquire about Mrs. Greenlease. She was stunned to learn that Mrs. Greenlease wasn't a patient. A call to the Greenlease home confirmed that Bobby's mother was well. It also confirmed that Bobby had been kidnapped. Mrs. Greenlease notified her husband who, in turn, told police. The cops called the F.B.I.

By that time Bobby was dead.

Next day the first ransom note arrived. Signed "M," it said in part:

Your boy been kidnapped. get $600,000 in $20's—$10's—Fed. Res. notes from all twelve districts. we realize it takes a few days to get that amount. Boy will be in good hands—when you have money ready put ad in K.C. Star. M—will meet you in Chicago next Sunday—Signed Mr G.

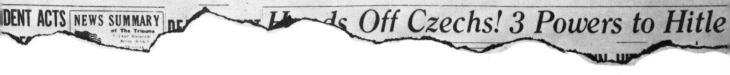

IDNAPER OF ROSS GETS CHAIR

DENT ACTS | **NEWS SUMMARY** *of The Tribune*   H—ds Off Czechs! 3 Powers to Hitle

John Henry Seadlund, half smiling after being condemned to the electric chair in Chicago, snaps his fingers in contempt. He had pleaded guilty to the kidnap slaying of Charles S. Ross.

Bobby Greenlease

Do not call police or try to use chemicals on bills or take numbers. Do not try to use any radio to catch us or boy dies. If you try to trap us your wife your other child and yourself will be killed you will be watched all the time. You will be told later how to contact us with money. When you get this note let us know by driving up and down main St. between 39 and 29 for 20 minutes with white rag on car aeriel.

If do exactly as we say an try no tricks, your boy will be back safe withen 24 hrs—after we check money

Deliver money in army duefel bag. Be ready to deliver at once on contact—
$400,000 in 20's
$200,000 in 10's

The size of the ransom was enough to divert the press and the public from the pursuit of the Red Menace, although some citizens wondered if the kidnapping wasn't a Red plot to destroy faith in local law enforcement.

Telephone calls from the mysterious "M" followed up the letter. The F.B.I. reconstructed one such conversation between "M" and Mrs. Greenlease as follows:

Mrs. Greenlease: M, this is Mrs. Greenlease.
M: Speaking.
Mrs. G: We have the money but we must know our boy is alive and well. Can you give me that? Can you give me anything that will make me know that?
M: A reasonable request, but to be frank with you the boy has been just about to drive us crazy. We couldn't risk taking him to a phone.
Mrs. G: Well, I can imagine that. Would you do this? Would you ask him two questions? Give me the answer to two questions?
M: Speaking.
Mrs. G: If I had the answer to these two questions I would know my boy is alive.
M: All right.
Mrs. G: Ask him what is the name of our driver in Europe this summer.
M: All right.
Mrs. G: And the second question, what did you build with your monkey blocks in your playroom the last night you were home . . . If I can get those answers from you, I'll know you have him and he is alive, which is the thing you know that I want.

M: We have the boy. He is alive. Believe me. He's been driving us nuts.

Mrs. G: Well, I can imagine that. He's such an active youngster.

M: He's been driving us nuts.

Mrs. G: Could you get those answers?

M: All right.

But, of course, "M" couldn't get those answers. When asked for them in another conversation, "M" replied:

"No . . . I couldn't . . . we didn't get anything from him."

The affair dragged on. So many notes and so many phone calls were received that confusion resulted. The $600,000, all eighty-five pounds of it, was left out in the country one day and the kidnappers couldn't find it. Finally, on October 4, 1953, at a highway bridge near Kansas City, the money was picked up.

A short time later "M" was back on the phone to assure the family that Bobby would be released within twenty-four hours. Moreover, said the voice, "We will certainly be glad to send him back."

But, of course, he couldn't come back alive.

No "miracle" of scientific detection solved the Greenlease kidnapping. Two days after the ransom was paid, the kidnappers were arrested by St. Louis police. Like the kidnappers of Willie Whitla, they went out to celebrate. Their only precaution was to travel to St. Louis before they got happily stoned. A cab driver got suspicious and tipped the cops. Carl A. Hall and his girl friend, Bonnie B. Heady, were picked up immediately.

Hall was thirty-four, the degenerate son of a respected attorney. On April 24, 1953, he had been paroled from prison after serving sixteen months of a five-year sentence for robbery. Ironically, he had robbed cab drivers.

Shortly after getting out he met Bonnie, seven years his senior, and at her invitation moved into her house at St. Joseph. There, between drinks, they planned the kidnapping of Bobby Greenlease.

Hall confessed shortly after police arrested

While classmates of slain Bobby Greenlease mourn for him, the American flag at his school is lowered to half mast.

(Above) The two kidnappers of Bobby
Greenlease, Bonnie Heady and
Carl Austin Hall.
(Left) The boy's classmates pray
for his safe return.
(Opposite page top) Uncovering the
body of Bobby Greenlease from its
shallow grave at the rear of a house
in St. Joseph, Missouri.

POST-DISPATCH

LOUIS, MONDAY, OCTOBER 12, 1953—40 PAGES

PRICE 5 CE

HALL, MRS. HEADY CONFESS KILLING GREENLEASE BOY

HALL SENT $500 TO ATTORNEY IN LETTER TO PAY RENTAL ON AUTO

FBI Intercepts Missive at St. Joseph, Has Lawyer Open

FBI Search at Scene of Child's Murder

ADMIT THEY DUG GRAVE FOR HIM IN HER YARD BEFORE KIDNAPING LAD, 6

Warrants Issued Under Lindbergh Law After Man Tells of Taking Victim Into Kansas, Shooting Him.

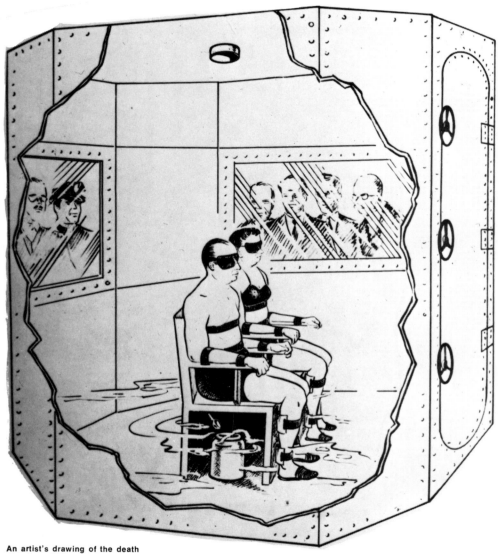

An artist's drawing of the death
chamber of Missouri State Prison and
how Heady and Hall looked as they
faced execution for the Greenlease
kidnap and slaying.

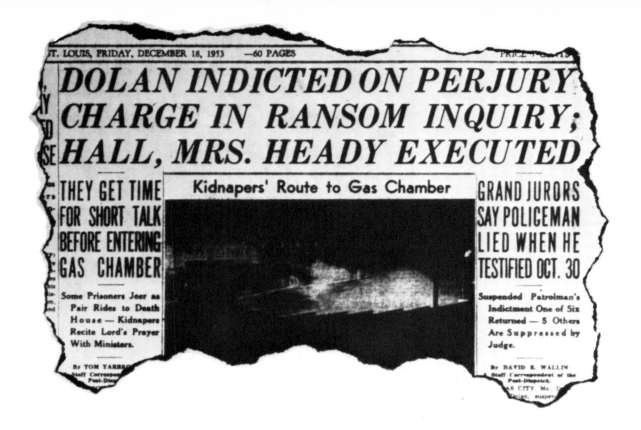

him. And even police veterans shuddered as he told his tale. Upon picking up Bonnie and Bobby in the station wagon, he had driven twelve miles out into the country. On an isolated road he stopped. Bonnie walked out into the field while Hall began strangling the small boy with his fingers. But, as Mrs. Greenlease had remarked, Bobby was "an active youngster" and wouldn't stand still for strangling. Hall was forced to pull out a revolver and shoot the boy in the head in order to kill him. He fired two shots. One of the slugs was later dug out of the station wagon which was found on a north Kansas City parking lot.

It was a mechanical pencil bearing the name of the Greenlease Cadillac agency that helped pinpoint the exact site of the murder. The pencil belonged to Bobby.

After the killing, the boy's body was taken to Bonnie's home in St. Joseph where the grave was ready beside the house. Hall dumped lime over the body and then covered it with soil. Later the couple planted flowers in the soft earth above the body.

A search of the apartment at 5316 Pershing Avenue, St. Louis, where Hall was arrested, uncovered $295,140 of the ransom money. Where was the rest of it? That question remains unanswered. Hall and Bonnie didn't know.

Bonnie was later quoted as saying she'd rather be dead than poor. She got her wish. On December 18, 1953, Hall and Bonnie went to the gas chamber at the Jefferson City State Penitentiary. Bonnie lived twenty seconds longer than her friend.

Another throwback to the old days was the kidnapping on July 4, 1956, of Peter Weinberger, an infant of thirty-three days. He was stolen from his carriage parked on the patio of his parents' home at Westbury, Long Island. When Mrs. Morris Weinberger went out to check her baby she found the carriage empty except for a note demanding $2,000 for the baby's return.

121

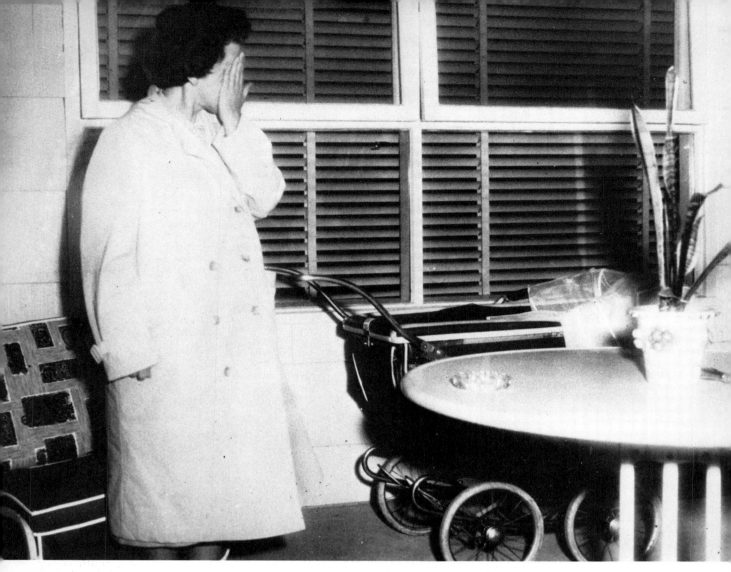

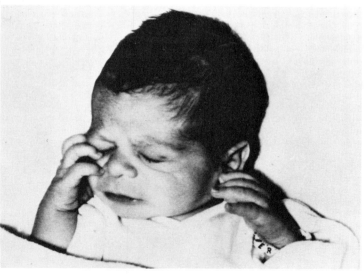

(Above) Mrs. Betty Weinberger weeps
on the porch of her home with the
empty baby carriage in view.
(Below) Her one-month-old baby,
Peter, taken from the carriage July 4.
A ransom note was found in
the carriage.

122

Journal American

m Hungary

Budapest Report on Page 16

No. 24,933—DAILY   FRIDAY, JULY 6, 1956   5 CENTS

SPORTS COMPLETE

Has This Mother's Plea Been Answered?

'KIDNAPER' PHONES FATHER

Eisenhower Decides ... Unit ... Bill

Mother Is Hopeful As Call Comes In

BULLETIN
Report New Contact With Peter's Abductor

Representatives of Mr. and Mrs. Morris Weinberg of Westbury, L. I., were reported late today to have made personal contact with the kidnaper of their month-old son, Peter, following an earlier telephone call in which the ransom demand...

Days of anguish followed for the Weinbergers as various hoaxers got into the act and tried to extort large sums. The New York press, or some of it, was blamed by officials for adding to the confusion with big headlines and sensational sob stories. Typical of the play given was that in the New York *Journal American* of July 8. A double banner headline across the top of the page read:

Kidnap Call To Family:
'I'll Be in Touch Again'

Down the right side of the page went the lead story in double column type. In the center of the page was a three column picture of Mrs. Weinberger appealing to the kidnapper to return her baby. Below it was a story describing the mother's anguish.

There was other news on the front page, but not much. One story concerned Arthur Miller, playwright and "recent bridegroom of Marilyn Monroe," who was refusing to tell the House UnAmerican Activities Committee about Communists he had known in 1939.

And since the *Journal American* was a Hearst newspaper, there was an "Editor's Report" by William Randolph Hearst, Jr., on the front page. Hearst, uncle of Patricia, was concerned not with kidnapping but with the threat of "security risks" in government jobs.

The F.B.I. ended much of the confusion on August 22, when it arrested Angelo John LaMarca, an ex-bootlegger. The clue to his identity was said to be his handwriting on the ransom note which matched his handwriting on file in a 1954 liquor case. LaMarca confessed. He said he had gone to the Weinberger home with the baby on the day after the kidnapping to collect the ransom, but was scared off by the crowds he saw in the area. He decided, instead, to abandon the baby and did so, leaving it alive near Exit 37 of Northern State Parkway near Plainview. It was dead when found there the next day by the F.B.I.

In December a state jury found LaMarca guilty of kidnapping and murder. It did not recommend mercy, thereby making a death sentence mandatory. After several stays of

Attention

I'm sorry this had to happen, but I am in bad need of money, & couldn't get it any other way.

Don't tell anyone or go to the Police about this, because I am watching you closely. I am scared stiff, & will kill the baby, at your first wrong move.

Just put $2000 "xxx" (two thousand) in small bills in a brown envelope, & place it next to the sign Post at the corner of Albemarle Rd. & Park Ave. at Exactly 10 o'clock tomorrow (Thursday) morning. If everything goes smooth, I will bring the baby back & leave him on the same corner "Safe & Happy" at exactly 12 noon.

No excuses, I can't wait!

Your baby sitter.

The F.B.I. had checked nearly two million records when it found that the handwriting on the Weinberger ransom note matched the handwriting in a probation file.
(Right) Arrest pictures of Angelo John LaMarca, the convicted kidnapper.

UNITED STATES PROBATION SYSTEM
MONTHLY REPORT

To: Angelo LaMarca
Print your name here

Date 5-4-56

This is my report for the month of April

I live at 154 B. Beach 116th St.
Street and apartment number or box and route number

Rockaway Park N.Y. Gl. 46497
City or town   Zone   State   Telephone

I work for Elmont Cab Co.
Name of person or company

5 Meacham Ave. Elmont, N.Y.
Address

as a Mechanic
Laborer, farmer, etc.

I worked 13 days this month. I have not worked full time because I closed my business (Angie's Service Station

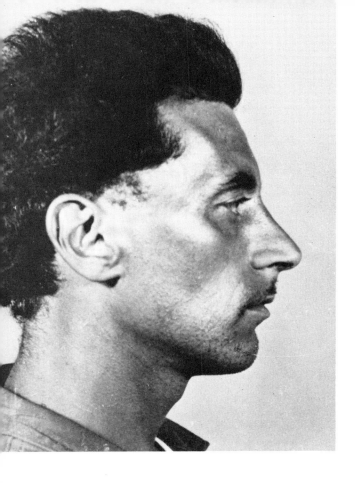

LaMarca Mercy Denied 'So It Will Not Happen Again'

By CHARLES ROLAND

Jurors in the Weinberger baby kidnap-murder case explained yesterday why they decided on no recommendation for mercy in declaring Angelo John LaMarca "guilty as charged."

Had their verdict contained the recommendation, LaMarca could have escaped death in Sing Sing's electric chair, the mandatory sentence.

LaMarca, 31, married and father of two children, will be sentenced next Friday to die by Judge Mario Pittoni, in the same Mineola, L. I., courtroom where the jury heard the case.

"LaMarca showed no mercy; he will get none, not just to punish him, but so that no such thing can happen again," the jurors agreed.

ABDUCTION FROM PATIO

Last July 4 LaMarca abducted 32-day-old Peter, son of Mr. and Mrs. Morris Weinberger, from the patio of their home, 17 Albermarle rd., Westbury, L. I., leaving in the baby carriage a ransom note demanding $2,000.

LaMarca never called to collect the money. He left Peter in a honeysuckle thicket off Exit 37 of Northern State pkwy., Plainview, where the baby was found dead the day after LaMarca was arrested on Aug. 27.

John W. Connelly, 46, the jury foreman, a telephone installer who lives with his wife and four children at 53 Park blvd., Malverne, L. I., told the N. Y. Journal-American what transpired in the six hours and 24 minutes the jurors, all fathers, deliberated. He said:

"The 12 of us searched our souls. We bent over backwards to give the defendant every break in the world.

"As we discussed the matter of mercy, we thought in particular about LaMarca's wife and children. We were not in a mood to be vindictive. We were here to be ju...

Push Surgery

execution, LaMarca died in the electric chair at Sing Sing on August 8, 1958. Behind he left a lot of bitterness. In an effort to prevent future bungling, Congress changed the Lindbergh Law to permit the F.B.I. to enter a kidnap case within twenty-four hours instead of seven days. For practical purposes, of course, the waiting time had varied from situation to situation—unofficially. Today, despite the legal waiting period, there is, again unofficially, practically no delay in cases that seem important.

Kidnappings continued on a regular basis, and at least to the principals, all of them were important. None, however, was sufficiently dramatic to tug at the heart-strings of the nation until more than a decade passed. Then the case of Barbara Jane Mackle added new refinements to ancient terror.

In December 1968, Barbara was a student at Emory University in Atlanta; she was the daughter of one of Miami's richest and most powerful men. Robert Francis Mackle, with his two brothers, built homes, hotels and cities throughout the state; friends and neighbors on Key Biscayne were such notables as Bebe Rebozo and President-Elect Richard M. Nixon. Barbara, however, had never thought of her family as being rich—for her things had always been, well, comfortable.

However, she had not been so comfortable that December. The autumn quarter had ended and final exams were under way. Worse, everyone had the flu. An epidemic was raging across the country and the infirmary at Emory was full. Her mother had flown to Atlanta, and rented a room with twin double beds at the Rodeway Inn near the campus. Barbara drove over and the mother began treating her twenty-year-old daughter. Four days passed. Barbara took some exams, arranged to take others later. She was still stuffed up, unable to breathe easily.

Tuesday morning, December 17, arrived. Barbara was having trouble sleeping. Both

Barbara Jane Mackle (above). (Opposite page) Her father, Robert F. Mackle.

126

Fla. Tycoon's Daughter, 20, Is Kidnaped

By HELEN DUDAR

The 20-year-old daughter of a multi-millionaire Florida land developer reportedly was kidnaped in her nightgown from an Atlanta motel early today by a young man and a boy armed with a shotgun.

The victim, Barbara Jane Mackle, a junior at Emory University there, had been ill with the flu and had been staying at the Roadway Inn in nearby DeKalb County with her mother, Jane. The kidnaping was reported to police by Mrs. Mackle, who said she was chloroformed by the two kidnapers.

The girl is the daughter of Robert F. Mackle, who, with two brothers, owns one of the biggest real estate development firms in the country. Their holdings include the Key Biscayne Hotel, where President-elect Nixon has often stayed.

Mrs. Mackle told DeKalb County police that the kidnap pair had clapped a chloroform-soaked cloth over her face and left her bound and gagged in her room at about 4 a.m. today. She freed herself after five minutes and called police.

Ransom Not Mentioned

No mention of ransom was made in the police report on the case. However, DeKalb Det. Capt. J. L. Smith said Mrs. Mackle had been "told what to do" by the kidnapers.

The FBI in Atlanta reported: "We're investigating the complaint." Federal agents were reported to have made strong protests over the DeKalb police report of the case, shutting off all further information.

The girl, a tall, willowy brunette, became ill a week ago and her mother flew to tend her. The Mackles's son, Robert Jr., student at the University of Pennsylvania Wharton School of Finance, is home in Coral [Gables,] Fla., on his Christmas [vacation.] [Th]e father flew to

Associated Press Wirephoto
ROBERT MACKLE
Missing girl's dad.

[com]panion had been a boy who had not seemed older than 12 years.

A cloth saturated with chloroform was placed over her face by the gunman, who told her to turn around, she related. Then the young boy tied her hands and feet with a white cord and put adhesive tape over her mouth. She said she then fainted.

The occupants of the adjoining room told police they had heard what had "sounded like a struggle" coming from the Mackle premises, but had seen nothing.

The father and his brothers Frank and Elliott own vast tracts of Florida land that they gradually have converted into lush money-making resort playlands.

Retirement Community

Among their developments are Deltona, a recently built retirement community between Daytona Beach and Orlando, and [Marco] Island, a luxury holiday [resort on the] Gulf of Mexico.

128

(Left) Barbara Jane Mackle in her
coffin-like box, in a photo taken
by her kidnapper.
(Above) The box in which she lived
for 80 hours.

The gaping hole in a pine forest near Atlanta from which Barbara Jane Mackle's coffin-like prison was taken.
(Right) One of her kidnappers, Gary Steven Krist, in custody.

women awoke, talked. It was 3 A.M. Barbara dozed.

There was a knock on the door.

A man's voice answered Mrs. Mackle's inquiry. He reported that a boy had been hurt in a wreck and was in the hospital asking for her. Assuming the boy was Stewart Woodward, Barbara's friend, Mrs. Mackle unhooked the door. The man put his shoulder against it and battered it open. He had a gun.

Barbara awoke as the man entered. Behind him was a smaller figure, a boy, thought Barbara. She was wrong. Mrs. Mackle decided the intruders were robbers. She told them to take the money and jewelry and leave. The "boy" forced the older woman down on the bed and held a cloth to her face. Barbara could smell chloroform. Her mother suddenly ceased to struggle.

Barbara, wearing only a nightgown and panties, was led out into the night. A car, its motor running, was waiting. She was pushed into the back seat and forced to lie down with her head in the "boy's" lap. She was cold.

The car went on and on. Barbara decided she had been kidnapped, then rejected the idea. Kidnapping was for children. They bumped over railroad tracks. A few minutes later the car stopped.

Conversation. The man confirmed that this was a kidnapping and he explained that he was going to put her under ground. She would be safe, he insisted, if she obeyed instructions and didn't try to break out. If she tried she might cause water to run into her "capsule"—or ants.

It made little sense. The girl, cold and scared, tried to appeal to the man. He was insistent. His companion, whom Barbara by now knew was a rather kind girl, kept promising to check every two hours to make sure all was well.

They carried Barbara, after injecting her with a hypodermic needle, across some open ground to a grassy knoll and placed her on her back. A cardboard sign was put beneath her chin and a picture taken with a Polaroid

camera. The sign said: "Kidnapped."

She was conscious when she was stuffed into a wooden box. Again came a rattle of instructions about air vents, water hoses, fans. It didn't make much sense. She screamed as the lid was closed over her, as screws were tightened, as the sound of dirt falling on top of the box gradually became muffled and died away.

"I'm in my casket," she thought.

She was to remain there for eighty-three hours.

While Barbara was being buried alive, her mother regained consciousness and freed herself from the tape which had liberally but sloppily been wound about her arms and legs. She called police. DeKalb County police arrived quickly but were reluctant to take the matter seriously. Where a coed in a motel was concerned, they had preconceived ideas despite the presence of a distraught mother. Stewart Woodward, the boy friend, came quickly when he was called and he put through a call to Robert Mackle on Key Biscayne. Mackle told him to call the F.B.I. He obeyed. The first agent to arrive wanted to know if there was money in the family. Mrs. Mackle replied evasively. The boy friend did not. Meanwhile, Robert Mackle caught a 7:15 A.M. flight to Atlanta. Two hours and fifteen minutes after it took off, the telephone rang at the Mackle home. A friend was waiting. The message was brief:

"Tell him to look under a palm tree in the northeast corner of the house—under a rock about six inches down."

During the period of this frenzied activity, Barbara Mackle made adjustments. Hysteria vanished and she explored her narrow home. She found a pillow and a box of Kotex. Under the box were some papers—a message. There was light enough to read:

DO NOT BE ALARMED. YOU ARE SAFE. YOU ARE PRESENTLY INSIDE A FIBERGLASS REINFORCED PLYWOOD CAPSULE BURIED BENEATH THE GROUND

Ruth Eisemann-Schier (above) after she was arrested in Norman, Oklahoma.

132

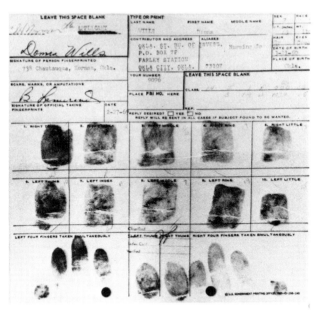

(Top) Note left by Ruth Eisemann-Schier in Oklahoma. It was comparison of her handwriting on the application (below) which she made as a carhop in Norman, Oklahoma, that led to her arrest.

The impounded Volvo and boat used in the Mackle case. The ransom money was found in the car after a police chase.

NEAR THE HOUSE IN WHICH YOUR KIDNAPPERS ARE STAYING. YOUR STATUS WILL BE CHECKED APPROXIMATELY EVERY TWO HOURS.

THE CAPSULE IS QUITE STRONG. YOU WILL NOT BE ABLE TO BREAK IT OPEN. BE ADVISED, HOWEVER, THAT YOU ARE BENEATH THE WATER TABLE. IF YOU SHOULD BREAK OPEN A SEAM YOU WOULD DROWN BEFORE WE COULD DIG YOU OUT. THE CAPSULE INSTRUMENTATION CONTAINS A WATER SENSITIVE SWITCH WHICH WILL WARN US IF THE WATER ENTERS THE CAPSULE TO A DANGEROUS DEGREE.

YOUR LIFE DEPENDS ON THE AIR DELIVERED TO YOUR CHAMBER VIA THE VENTILATION FAN. THIS FAN IS POWERED BY A LEAD-ACID STORAGE BATTERY CAPABLE OF SUPPLYING THE FAN MOTOR WITH POWER FOR 270 HOURS. HOWEVER, THE USE OF THE LIGHT AND OTHER SYSTEMS FOR ONLY A FEW HOURS COUPLED WITH THE HIGHER AMPERAGE DRAIN WILL REDUCE THIS FIGURE TO ONLY ONE WEEK OF SAFETY.

SHOULD THE AIR SUPPLIED PROVE TO BE TOO MUCH YOU CAN PARTLY BLOCK THE AIR OUTLET WITH A PIECE OF PAPER. A MUFFLER HAS BEEN PLACED IN THE AIR PASSAGE TO PREVENT ANY NOISE YOU MAKE FROM REACHING THE SURFACE: IF WE DETECT ANY COMMOTION WHICH WE FEEL IS DANGEROUS, WE WILL INTRODUCE ETHER TO THE AIR INTAKE AND PUT YOU TO SLEEP.

THE FAN OPERATES ON 6 VOLTS. IT HAS A SWITCH WITH TWO POSITIONS TO SWITCH BETWEEN THE TWO AVAILABLE CIRCUITS. SHOULD ONE CIRCUIT FAIL TURN TO THE OTHER.

THE BOX HAS A PUMP WHICH WILL EVACUATE ANY ACCIDENTAL LEAKAGE FROM THE BOX WHEN YOU TURN THE PUMP SWITCH ON TO THE "ON" POSITION. THIS PUMP USES 15 TIMES AS MUCH POWER AS YOUR VENTILATION FAN (7.5 AMPS); YOUR LIFE SUPPORT BATTERY WILL NOT

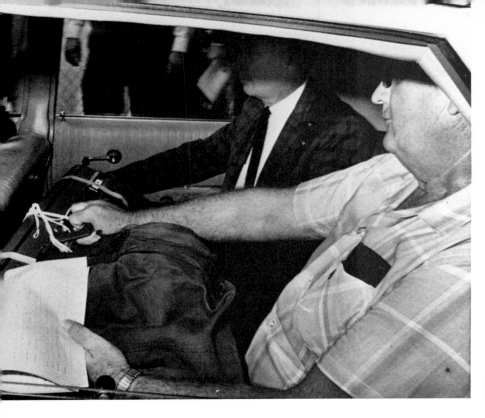

A suitcase containing an estimated $500,000 found in the car.

ALLOW USE OF THE PUMP EXCEPT FOR EMERGENCY WATER EVACUATION.

THE LIGHT USES 2.5 TIMES THE AMPERAGE OF THE AIR CIRCULATION SYSTEM. USE OF THE LIGHT WHEN NOT NECESSARY WILL CUT YOUR BATTERY SAFETY MARGIN SUBSTANTIALLY. IF YOU USE THE LIGHT CONTINUOUSLY YOUR LIFE EXPECTANCY WILL BE CUT TO ONE THIRD OF THE WEEK WE HAVE ALLOTTED YOU BEFORE YOU ARE RELEASED.

YOUR CAPSULE CONTAINS A WATER JUG WITH THREE GALLONS OF WATER AND A TUBE FROM WHICH TO DRINK IT. BE CAREFUL TO BLOW THE WATER FROM THE TUBE WHEN YOU ARE FINISHED DRINKING TO AVOID SIPHONING THE WATER ONTO THE FLOOR WHEN THE TUBE END DROPS BELOW THE WATER LEVEL.

YOUR CAPSULE CONTAINS A BUCKET FOR REFUSE AND THE PRODUCTS OF YOUR BOWEL MOVEMENTS. THE BUCKET HAS AN ANTIBACTERIAL SOLUTION IN IT: DON'T TIP IT OVER. THE LID SEALS TIGHTLY TO PREVENT THE ESCAPE OF ODORS. A ROLL OF WAX PAPER IS PROVIDED—USE IT TO PREVENT SOLID WASTE FROM CONTAMINATING YOUR BED. KOTEX IS PROVIDED SHOULD YOU NEED IT.

BLANKETS AND A MAT ARE PROVIDED. YOUR WARMTH DEPENDS ON BODY HEAT SO REGULATE THE AIR TO PREVENT LOSS OF HEAT FROM THE CAPSULE.

A CASE OF CANDY IS PROVIDED TO FURNISH ENERGY TO YOUR BODY.

TRANQUILIZERS ARE PROVIDED TO AID YOU IN SLEEPING—THE BEST WAY YOU HAVE TO PASS THE TIME.

THE VENTILATION SYSTEM IS DOUBLY SCREENED TO PREVENT INSECTS OR ANIMALS FROM ENTERING THE CAPSULE AREA. YOU RISK BEING EATEN BY ANTS SHOULD YOU BREAK THESE PROTECTION SCREENS.

THE ELECTRICAL COMPONENTS BEHIND THESE SCREENS ARE DELICATE AND THEY SUPPORT YOUR LIFE. DON'T ATTEMPT TO TOUCH THESE CIRCUITS.

*WE'RE SURE YOUR FATHER WILL PAY
THE RANSOM WE HAVE ASKED IN LESS
THAN ONE WEEK. WHEN YOUR FATHER
PAYS THE RANSOM WE WILL TELL HIM
WHERE YOU ARE AND HE'LL COME FOR
YOU. SHOULD HE FAIL TO PAY WE WILL
RELEASE YOU, SO BE CALM AND REST—
YOU'LL BE HOME FOR CHRISTMAS ONE
WAY OR THE OTHER.*

The light, about the size of a Christmas-tree bulb, was in the top left-hand corner of the box. Barbara reached up and turned it off.

In Miami, meanwhile, as in Atlanta, the F.B.I. was in action. No nonsense about waiting twenty-four hours here. The Mackles were important people. Under a rock beneath the palm tree, an agent found the ransom note in a bottle. It was long, technical, and specific. Barbara was buried alive. If $500,000 was paid, she would be rescued in time. If there was delay, a doublecross, she might never be rescued. The Mackles were told to place an ad in Miami newspapers—"Loved one, please come home. We will pay all expenses and meet you anywhere at any time. Your Family." When the notice appeared, a post-midnight telephone call would reveal where the money should be delivered.

The Associated Press broke the story at 12:05 P.M. The tip had come from a DeKalb County police official. The F.B.I. refused to confirm, but various reporters soon identified the Mackles and established the validity of the tip. Details were lacking, however,

The First National Bank of Miami was asked to collect a half million dollars in $20 bills. It had the cash on hand and by 2 P.M. the "package" was ready for a small army of officials to record the serial numbers. With F.B.I. agents watching, the men worked late. Most of them didn't know why. Other agents arranged to run the ad in the *Miami Herald*. Reporter Jim Savage was asked to arrange for the ad to go in the edition after the signal was given that the money was ready. The *Herald*'s

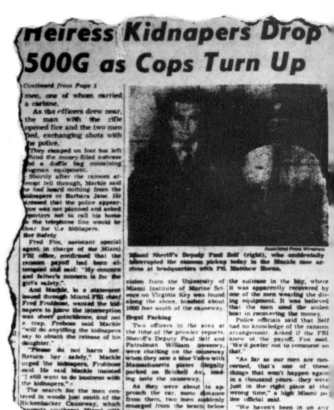

Heiress Kidnapers Drop 500G as Cops Turn Up

men, one of whom carried a carbine.

As the officers drew near, the man with the rifle opened fire and the two men fled, exchanging shots with the police.

They escaped on foot but left behind the money filled suitcase and a duffle bag containing frogman equipment.

Shortly after the ransom attempt fell through, Mackle said he had heard nothing from the kidnapers or Barbara Jane. He stressed that the police appearance was not planned and asked reporters not to call his home so the telephone line would be clear for the kidnapers.

Her Safety

Fred Fox, assistant special agent in charge of the Miami FBI office, confirmed that the ransom payoff had been attempted and said: "My concern and father's concern is for the girl's safety."

And Mackle, in a statement issued through Miami FBI chief Fred Frohbose, wanted the kidnapers to know the interception was sheer coincidence, and not a trap. Frobose said Mackle "will do anything the kidnapers say to obtain the release of his daughter."

"Please do not harm her. Return her safely," Mackle urged the kidnapers, Frohbose said. He said Mackle insisted "I still want to do business with the kidnapers."

The search for the men centered in woods just south of the Rickenbacker Causeway, which connects southeast Miami with Virginia Key and Key Biscayne, vacation headquarters of President-elect Nixon.

One of the men was described about 40, stocky, with dark—

The other was said to be young and about 25.

Through a snafu, according to Miami police, devel—

The woods, to the shore—

Miami Sheriff's Deputy Paul Self (right), who accidentally interrupted the ransom pickup today in the Mackle case arrives at headquarters with Ptl. Matthew Burns.

stolen from the University of Miami Institute of Marine Science on Virginia Key was found along the shore, beached about 1000 feet south of the causeway.

Illegal Parking

Two officers in the area at the time of the prowler reports, Sheriff's Deputy Paul Self and Patrolman William Sweeny, were chatting on the causeway when they saw a blue Volvo with Massachusetts plates illegally parked on Brickell Av., leading onto the causeway.

As they were about to approach the car, some distance from them, two men suddenly emerged from the beach below the causeway. One carried the suitcase and carbine. The second man carried the duffle bag.

Seeing the officers approaching, the men dropped the suitcase and bag and the man with the gun opened up on the cops. The men began to run toward the car and fled past it into the wooded area.

the suitcase in the bay, where it was apparently recovered by one of the men wearing the diving equipment. It was believed that the men used the stolen boat in recovering the money.

Police officials said that Self had no knowledge of the ransom arrangement. Asked if the FBI knew of the payoff, Fox said. "We'd prefer not to comment on that."

"As far as our men are concerned, that's one of those things that won't happen again in a thousand years—they were just in the right place at the wrong time," a high Miami police official said.

"We haven't been in on any part of the investigation in Atlanta or the things that developed here," Miami Police Chief Price said.

The girl had been abducted from a motel room she was sharing with her mother in Atlanta.

Price said the intervention by his officers resulted "because there was no coordination between us and the family or others."

Marvin Mathes, a caretaker park area, said a man a woman app—nish descent, had question—

Kidnaped Girl Home After $500,000 Is Paid

MIAMI, Dec. 21 (UPI) — Miss Barbara Jane Mackle, buried almost four days in a coffin-like box in North Georgia woods, returned home today in good condition after her father paid $500,000 ransom.

The safe return of the girl accomplished, the Federal Bureau of Investigation pressed a nationwide search for the suspected kidnapers, Gary Steven Krist, 23 years old, alias George Deacon, an escaped convict, and his friend, Miss Ruth Eisemann Schier, 26.

Both are employes at the University of Miami Institute of Marine Science. They were charged in federal warrants Thursday night.

Miss Mackle, 20 years old, a junior at Emory University in Atlanta, was found yesterday afternoon by FBI agents, apparently acting on directions given by the kidnapers after they received the payoff.

The FBI said in Washington that the girl had been found in an isolated, heavily wooded rural area about 20 miles northeast of Atlanta.

"She had been buried in coffin-like box 18 inches underground. The top of the box had been securely fastened screws and the box contained small battery unit and a fan two flexible vent pipes w protruded just above ground, the FBI said. "Th box contained a limited am of food and water and h small light which had fail some hours before the vi was located."

Buried 80 Hours

The FBI said she had be the box about 80 hours. She wearing her nightgown weater — wh Weather Bureau temperatu

skirt and a fur-collared coat, she boarded the plane for the flight to Florida.

Miss Mackle told her mother that in the more than 80 hours she lay in the box she worried most that her family was worrying about her.

Krist was added to the FBI's list of 10 most wanted fugitives. He escaped from a Tracy, Calif., prison in November 1966 by climbing over a fence with a fellow inmate. The other man was killed by guards in the escape attempt.

John Hurley of the Marine Institute said that Deacon, the name under which he knew Krist, was a "tough, pushy kind of fellow . . . (who) was always

TURN TO PAGE 8, COLUMN 1

*Winter o
As Li
F*

ace crime reporter, Savage knew instantly what was involved. But the F.B.I. had asked that the information be "off the record" and Savage agreed.

At last all was ready. The ad was in the paper. Seventy-five pounds of money stood waiting. An elaborate electronic hookup had been made to record incoming calls and to trace them. Scores of F.B.I. agents were stationed in fast cars all about Miami. In charge was an inspector from the "Seat of Government," as the aging Hoover described Washington, D.C. Hoover had sent him personally.

A dozen men waited in the Mackle home on the evening of December 18, waiting for the call, promised for after midnight, which would give directions for dropping the money. At 3:47 A.M. the call came.

The instructions were complicated. The "drop site" was isolated, hard to find. Robert Mackle tried to get more specific directions. He was afraid he'd get lost. He did. An hour was wasted before the money was left in the darkness. Meanwhile, the kidnapper had called back to discover what was wrong. He seemed less curt, somehow, as if he understood the problems and perhaps felt sorry for having caused them. He promised to check the designated location again. A little later the Mackles checked. The money was gone. Everyone felt elated. The carefully made plans had gone awry but if the kidnapper had the money perhaps Barbara might yet live.

Then came the bad news.

Local police, knowing only that Barbara Mackle had been kidnapped in Atlanta, found a deserted car on a deserted street. They staked it out, thinking that the occupant might be busy robbing a home nearby. A lot of homes were being robbed in Miami in those days, sometimes with police assistance. But these cops weren't crooks. They staked out the car. After a while they saw a man carrying a duffel bag approach. They decided to check him out. The man opened fire, then ran.

Behind him he left the huge bag. The cops opened it and saw the stacks and stacks of $20 bills. They figured someone had knocked off an armored car somewhere, so they took the money to headquarters and called the F.B.I.

And the news was out.

The abandoned car, a 1966 blue Volvo bearing Massachusetts license plates, proved to be a gold mine. It contained all kinds of evidence connecting it to the kidnapping, and it permitted the kidnappers to be identified. Apparently the kidnappers had been living out of it. There were even pictures—of the woman in bra and panties; of the man, bearded and beefy; and of Barbara Mackle with the "Kidnapped" sign under her chin.

The woman was identified as Ruth Eisemann-Schier, a former University of Miami student from Honduras. The man first identified as "George Deacon," was something of a wanderer. Later his real name, Gary Steven Krist, was established. A man who bought a small baggage trailer from a man and woman driving a blue Volvo heard about the police shootout on his radio, and he called the FBI. In the trailer some old letters addressed to Krist were found.

Now it was the evening of December 19. On television Bob Hope had a special about Santa Claus being kidnapped. Father Mulcahy, a Catholic priest, received a call from Krist. A new pickup site was described, one easier to find. The priest got it all down on paper. This time the drop was made and the money picked up without complications. Now everything depended on Krist. Would he keep his word? There was new information about him. As a boy he had served a year in a school for delinquents in Utah. On the routine IQ test he had scored an astounding 142. He was a genius. Later he had served time in California for car theft. In 1966 he had escaped.

At 12:47 P.M. the next day, December 20, Trisha Poindexter, a pretty brunette from Rome, Georgia, was on duty at the F.B.I.

switchboard in Atlanta. A man called with information on the Mackle kidnapping. He refused to talk to an agent. He spelled out precise directions. He mentioned a "capsule" near Norcross, some twenty-two miles northeast of Atlanta. Trisha wrote it all down, gave it to an agent. Within minutes a car was on its way and all the other F.B.I. cars waiting around Atlanta were ordered to follow.

Jack Keith was in charge. After one false try, they found a dirt road leading to a demolished house. The men began to hunt, walking rapidly about, looking for some sign.

Underground, Barbara Mackle heard a noise, a rustle. It was the first noise she had heard from outside her "casket." She started pounding on the top of the box.

Above ground Vincent Capazella heard a noise. Someone knocking. Robert Kennemur heard it too. They dropped to their knees and began to brush away the pine needles. They saw red clay. They shouted.

The girl heard the shout. She stopped pounding. She smiled.

With hands, buckets and sticks they pushed and pulled the earth back, ripped open the box and looked down on the girl. She was still smiling. She said:

"You're the handsomest men I've ever seen."

Director Hoover personally gave the good news to the Mackles in Miami.

The hunt began for Krist and his female companion. The trail was not hard to follow as Krist headed for the boondocks. Hard pressed, he abandoned a boat off Hog Island, west of Florida. In it was found a duffel bag containing $479,000 in $20 bills. A few hours later Krist was captured. "You might as well shoot me," he told his captors. "I'm a dead man anyway."

Ruth Eisemann-Schier was more elusive. The F.B.I. put her on its list of "Ten Most Wanted." She was the first woman to make it. When she found work at Central State

Hospital near Norman, Oklahoma, she submitted to fingerprinting as part of the routine. Five days later the F.B.I. nabbed her. Krist was sentenced to life imprisonment. Ruth got seven years.

The Mackle kidnapping was in many respects unique. Like Loeb and Leopold, Krist was intelligent. Unlike them, he executed his plan well. The foul-up in Miami when uninformed local police blundered into the case and captured his car had been the cause of his undoing. Or had Mackle found the drop site that night on schedule, Krist might never have been caught.

Times were changing—the Mackle case proved that styles were becoming more sophisticated, if nothing else. Already a new brand of politically motivated kidnapping was becoming popular, even more frightening, perhaps, than the greed-motivated ones of the past. The first case of the new generation was nine years old when Barbara Mackle was kidnapped. It involved international politics and the Old Testament code of revenge—an eye for an eye, a tooth for a tooth.

The story began in Nazi Germany. Adolf Eichmann, an ambitious young man who in his more innocent days had dated a Jewish girl, worked his way up to become the executive in charge of exterminating all Jews in Germany and in German-occupied Europe. Eichmann did not make the policy of the "Final Solution," but he carried it out with an attention to detail that left little doubt he approved of his task. In preparation for his work he studied Nazi racial theories and even learned to speak Hebrew.

Being realists, however, men like Eichmann became aware that the war was lost long before Hitler died in a Berlin bunker. They created an efficient "underground railroad" to help them find their way across Europe to Cairo or on across the Atlantic to Argentina. The latter was preferred since Dictator Juan Peron was a graduate of a German officers' school at Potsdam and was a great admirer

Eichmann (above) as a young man. (Right) The ovens at Buchenwald with human bones inside. Prisoners of all nationalities were burned to death here.

Israel Says Eichmann Left Voluntarily

Buenos Aires, June 7 (AP)—The Israeli government has confirmed that a determined band of "Jewish volunteers" tracked Adolf Eichmann to Argentina but insists that the ex-Gestapo official was not kidnaped but agreed to go to Israel to stand trial.

An Israeli note to the Argentine government told of a relentless 15-year quest that spanned three continents and ended with a showdown in Buenos Aires. Couched in mollifying terms, the note claimed that the group that caught up with Eichmann here and took him to Israel act...

Jews Guarded In Argentina

From Combined Cable Dispatches

Buenos Aires, June 1—At the Israeli Embassy, at Jewish business offices and at synagogues around the city, the police stood guard today.

There were no guards at the Eichmann house. Inside, Adolf Eichmann's ...

Auschwitz: Portrait of The Architect

By SID FRIEDLANDER

"... absolutely convinced that if he could succeed in destroying the biological basis of Jewry in the East by complete extermination, then Jewry as a whole would never recover from the blow.

"... completely obsessed with his mission ..."

This was Adolf Eichmann, as seen by one of his major henchmen, Rudolf Hoess, in his autobiography, "Commandant of Auschwitz."

"Eichmann was a vivacious, active man in his thirties, and always full of energy," wrote Hoess. "He was constantly hatching new plans and perpetually on the lookout for innovations and improvements. He could never rest. He was obsessed with the Jewish question and the order which had been given for its final solution."

A grotesque ... one murderer by another. Eichmann, the Nazi ... for the death of ... Jews and now, after ... ld for ... Hoess who admitted ... years ...

---

of Hitler and Nazism. He welcomed Nazi refugees.

Just before *Gotterdämmerung*, Eichmann was said to have estimated that he was responsible for the deaths of between five and six million Jews. He added, according to one of his associates, that "he would leap laughing into the grave because the feeling that he had five million people on his conscience would be for him a source of extraordinary satisfaction." Yet, for all his talk, Eichmann did not intend to die prematurely. He was only thirty-nine when the war ended. Picked up by American troops who did not understand his role and consequently were not as careful in guarding their prisoner as they might have been, he promptly escaped and vanished. The "underground railroad" sent him by easy stages to Rome which had become the main center of help for Nazi refugees.

Taking his time, making no move until all risks had been eliminated, Eichmann awaited his chance. It was five years after the Nazi surrender before he reached Buenos Aires in the summer of 1950. He traveled under a passport issued in Rome in the name of "Ricardo Klement," supposedly a central European of Latin-American origin. Once in Argentina, he secured the necessary papers that established him as a citizen, and began to make plans for his family to join him.

In Europe, however, Eichmann had not been forgotten. And as the full story of Hitler's "final solution" became known, there was renewed interest in locating the man most responsible for implementing it. Jewish investigators, some of them survivors of concentration camps, began the hunt. As far as they were concerned, Eichmann was "Jewish Enemy Number One."

The search was complicated by the fact that Eichmann had managed to destroy his personal papers and all official photographs. The hunters had no way of recognizing their quarry if they found him. Gradually the belief grew that he was dead.

(Above) The villa on Lake Hannsee in West Berlin where Eichmann met with high-ranking SS officers to decide the final solution of the ''Jewish problem.'' The decision was to systematically eradicate millions of European Jews.

One man who didn't think so was Manos Diamant, a Polish Jew who had fought in the underground during the war. He located Eichmann's family living in a rented house in Bad Aussee, a resort in central Austria. Diamant, moving cautiously, managed to become acquainted with a woman friendly with Mrs. Eichmann. Through her he became friendly with the family and became a constant visitor to the home. Discovering the Eichmanns badly wanted a maid but couldn't compete with the high wages paid by American officers, Diamant found them one they could afford. She was blonde enough to be an Aryan, but she was, in fact, a Jewish spy.

Despite this success, the gambit failed. Hunt as she would, the female spy was unable to find a photograph of Eichmann or a clue as to his whereabouts. But Diamant was undiscouraged. He withdrew his colleague and returned to Vienna where he located a former mistress of the missing Nazi. Whereas Mrs. Eichmann lived on hope, the mistress subsisted on memory. Posing as a Dutch ally of the Nazis, Diamant won her confidence. She enjoyed having someone with whom she could talk about the good old days. Finally, on impulse, she brought out a photograph album and opened it to a photograph of Eichmann in S.S. uniform.

The Jew had friends in official circles and he arranged for the woman's house to be raided—allegedly in a search for black-market goods. Nothing was found, of course, but the photograph of Eichmann disappeared from its album. The quarry could now be identified.

The photograph was turned over to Simon Wiesenthal, a civil engineer rescued by American troops from a concentration camp

Two studies of Adolf Eichmann during
his trial in Jerusalem: he ponders a
point and (right) he digs through
his notes.

144

near Linz. Following his release he joined the American war-crimes team which was seeking evidence to be used in prosecuting major Nazi figures. Eichmann became his special project. When, in 1947, Mrs. Eichmann petitioned to have her husband declared dead, Wiesenthal intervened to prevent it.

Yet no real clue to Eichmann's whereabouts was found. In 1952, Mrs. Eichmann took a train to Genoa, obtained visas for herself and her sons, and sailed to Argentina without being noticed. Belatedly Wiesenthal got on the trail and by the next year he had sufficient information to be sure the Eichmann tribe was in Argentina. Reports to that effect circulated in the press, but Eichmann was unworried. As long as the Argentine government protected him he was safe.

Six years passed. The State of Israel, born in conflict, was eleven years old when its secret agents learned in 1959 that a former highly placed Nazi, Dr. Johannes von Leer, was preparing to leave Cairo for South America. On the assumption that von Leer would immediately get in touch with former comrades upon arriving, it was decided to follow him closely.

In Buenos Aires von Leer saw a lot of people but one more than others. Eventually the Jews became convinced that "Ricardo Klement" was the man they wanted above all others. In the long interval of searching, Eichmann's fingerprints had been found. They were now compared to those on file for "Klement" and, of course, they matched.

Having run the fox to earth, the next question was what to do about it. Legally, Israel had no grounds on which to base an extradition request. The crimes Eichmann had committed took place before Israel was formed. Moreover, he was now a citizen of Argentina and, presumably, was in good standing. Legally, then, there seemed no way to gain possession of the man.

But the desire to demonstrate to the world that the Jewish state had the power to punish

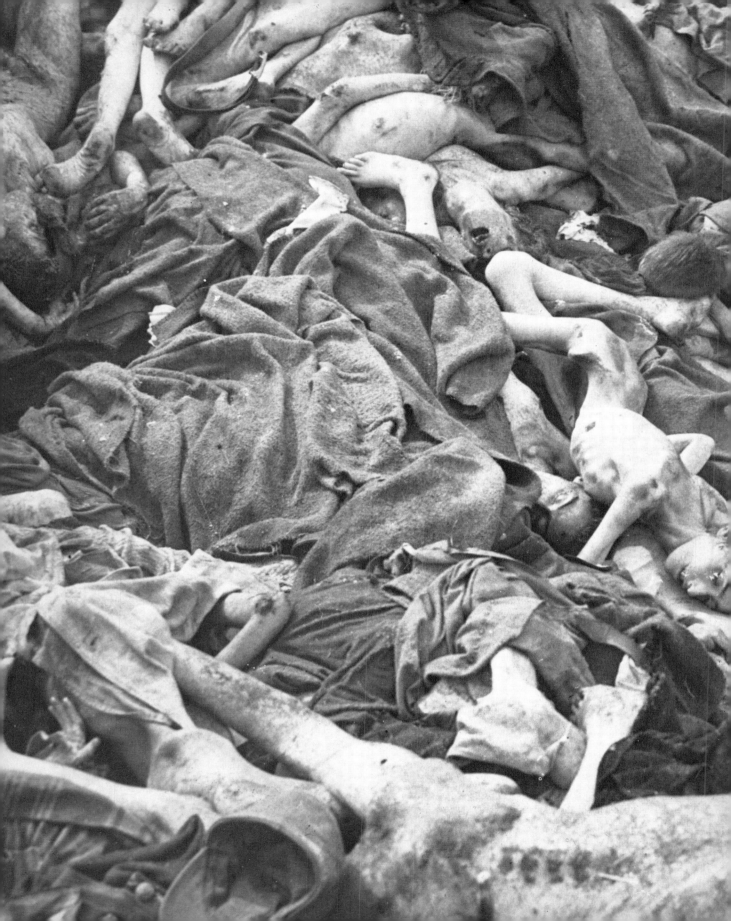

the former enemies of its people was too strong to quibble over legal technicalities. The problem soon boiled down to assassination or kidnapping. The latter was preferred because it would give Israel a chance to try Eichmann for his crimes and thus perhaps win moral authority for his execution.

A new team of secret agents, men and women, went to Argentina. As carefully as an Alvin Karpis plotting a kidnapping, the team studied Eichmann's personal habits. The big problem was not to seize him, but to get him safely out of the country without alerting Argentine authorities.

Early in 1960, the Israeli government received a routine invitation to send a special delegation to attend ceremonies marking the 150th anniversary of Argentina's freedom from Spanish rule. The latter part of May was designated as the period of celebration.

In Tel Aviv someone had a bright idea.

Reinforcements were sent to the secret agents in Argentina along with instructions to be ready to effect the "snatch" by mid-May. The government-owned airline was told to get one of its Britannias ready to fly to Buenos Aires. The city was not a regular stop for El Al, and much preparation was needed to assure the fifteen thousand-mile round trip could be safely made.

Meanwhile, Israeli agents noticed that every Tuesday evening Eichmann left the Buenos Aires plant where he worked and took a bus to his son's house for dinner. After dinner he usually walked home alone. It was decided to grab him when he left his son's house.

Somehow communications from Israel became a problem, and the kidnapping took place a week earlier than planned. Eichmann was strolling along the dark street, his stomach full of rich food and beer, when a dark limousine drew up beside him. Three armed men got out and politely ordered him into the car. Eichmann didn't seemed too alarmed at first, apparently assuming Peron's secret police wanted to talk to him about something. But

(Above) Grimfaced Servatius, listening to the prosecution during the trial.
(Top, opposite page) Yaakov Viernik, seventy-two, a Polish-born carpenter who related how 750,000 Jews were killed and their bodies stripped of gold fillings and teeth which were shipped to Berlin.
(Below, opposite page) Mrs. Liona Noiman shows the bullet scars she received during her escape from the Nazis. Fifteen hundred of her compatriots from Latvia froze to death or were shot en route from Riga, Latvia.

abruptly he stiffened. Assuming he had recognized them as Jews, one of the captors left no doubt. Speaking in German, he said: "Herr Eichmann, you are going to account for your sins."

The prisoner was taken to a rented villa and kept under 24-hour guard. There was fear he might kill himself. After some persuasion, the details of which were never publicized, Eichmann signed a document agreeing to be transferred to Israel and there to stand trial. It was another attempt to give legitimacy to the whole affair. Meanwhile, a cablegram was sent to the Israeli Secret Service. It said simply, "Beast in chains."

The Israeli airliner arrived on May 20, carrying the diplomats expected for the anniversary celebration. It also carried a larger crew than usual, all of whom were hungry. The diplomats went their way and the crew drove into town to eat while the plane was refueled and prepared for the return flight. Unfortunately it couldn't wait for the ceremonies to end; it was needed elsewhere.

Eichmann, who didn't know what his captors were waiting for, ate his usual dinner that night in the villa where he was being held. Not usual was the drug placed in his coffee. Soon he was in a stupor—not unconscious but oblivious to events around him. The "special members" of the crew collected him and returned to the plane. To the Argentine officials on duty he appeared drunk. No suspicion was aroused as the crew climbed aboard and began preparations for departure. Everything was done according to regulations. Indeed, the regular crew didn't realize there was any need for speed.

The plane headed for Dakar on the coast of West Africa. The French who controlled it had no love for Nazis. Then came the dangerous flight across the sands of the Sahara Desert to Tel Aviv. The landing there was made on the afternoon of May 21, the plane parking in a remote corner of the field. Two days later Prime Minister David Ben-Gurion,

149

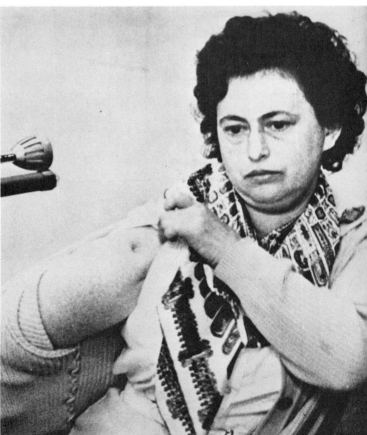

white-haired and proud, rose in the Israeli Parliament to announce the "arrest" of Adolf Eichmann. Much of the world was delighted— at first.

The "trial" of Eichmann began the following year after long preparation. In effect, the Israelis were trying not just Eichmann but the policies and practices of Adolf Hitler. The outcome was never in doubt as the magnitude of the Nazi crime against humanity was documented by tattooed survivors of Dachau, Buchenwald and Sachsenhausen in horrible detail. By comparison, the Israeli kidnapping of Eichmann seemed a minor matter indeed— and perhaps that reaction was also planned.

On December 15, 1961, Eichmann was sentenced to hang for crimes against—not Israel, not even the Jewish people—but humanity. And on May 31, 1963, he was hanged. He was given no opportunity to go laughing to his grave, for in a final bit of Old Testament justice his body was cremated even as millions of Jews in Germany had been cremated. His ashes were scattered in the Mediterranean Sea to avoid polluting the soil of Israel.

As one English writer put it, those who regretted both the kidnapping and the trial of Eichmann "were applying Christian standards to a nation whose philosophy and creed is older and more primitive than the revolutionary teachings of Christ."

But the cycle did not end with Eichmann. His had been a political kidnapping, and in the years that followed the practice spread. Soon it wasn't necessary to justify such crimes in the name of humanity—nationalism and then political expediency sufficed. The hijackings of airlines loaded with passengers became commonplace in the Middle East as the code of an eye for an eye provoked reaction and retaliation. The murder of Israeli athletes at the Olympic Games in Munich in 1972 was but an outgrowth of the philosophy that excused the ritual murder of Eichmann.

The poison spread to South America where political kidnappings of American diplomats and businessmen became almost routine methods for raising funds and gaining the release of prisoners. Handbooks were published for urban guerrillas in which kidnapping was listed as one of several "methods of action." Another such "method" was bank robbery. Ultimately the poison reached the United States, where the first to be affected was a young woman named Patricia Hearst.

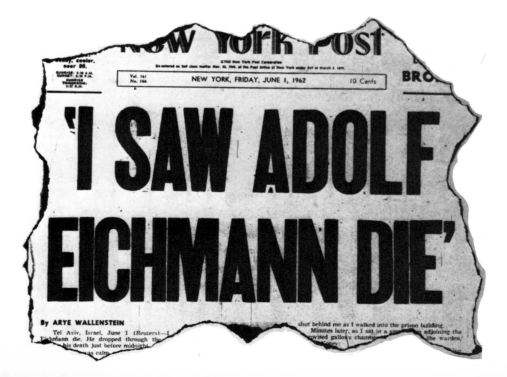

6. THE REVOLUTION COMES

The cesspool of Watergate, kept desperately dammed until President Nixon's re-election in 1972, began leaking shortly after he was inaugurated in 1973. Like a dark stain, a sense of outrage, of betrayal, spread across the nation, bring with it a growing cynicism and a distrust of authority at all levels.

Economic conditions added to the political woes—woes compounded when the Vice President of the United States, Spiro T. Agnew, did some plea bargaining and saved himself a jail sentence by resigning. Inflation became a monster, attacking Americans where it hurt. Climaxing a bad year, the "Oil Crisis" was announced—and many people thought it a hoax.

Things were so bad that a good kidnapping might almost have been welcomed as a change of pace, an opportunity to feel sorry for someone else for a change. But, while kidnappings increased in number, nothing unique occurred. There was only the Getty case in Italy and it was interesting only because it involved the grandson of the world's richest man.

Eugene Paul Getty II, known around Rome as "The Golden Hippie," was at sixteen years old a strange blend of arrogance and humility, of naïveté and pride. He was in the custody of his mother, Gail, who had divorced his father and remarried. The father lived in London, avoiding police questions about his second wife's death. Over all in the background was the miserly figure of the boy's grandfather, multi-millionaire Jean Paul Getty, still making money at eighty-one years, and very much a legend.

Young Paul, as he was known to his friends, lived the life of a "Jet-Set" brat. At sixteen, he was used to having what he wanted in women, motorcycles, and drugs. He was, as he himself put it, "an awful snot." For now he lived off his mother; somewhere in the future he would inherit a trust fund, a lot of money. That fact gave him status, made him important to the hippie set in Rome.

On June 10, after a night on the town, he bought a newspaper and a Mickey Mouse comic book and started home. He was pretty drunk. A big car came along, men with guns

Eugene Paul Getty II, grandson of oil billionaire J. Paul Getty. (Many news articles gave the boy's first name incorrectly.)

got out and hit him over the head. They put him in the car and drove for hours. After a while Getty realized he had been kidnapped.

The trouble was no one believed it. Neither his mother, his grandfather, the police, nor the readers of newspapers. The story got some play in the United States because of the Getty fortune, but it looked like another hoax. The theory was that the youth had arranged the caper to get more spending money.

Getty was taken to the "toe" of the Italian "boot," an area called Calabria. The land there is poor, the people are poor and the "Mainland Mafia" rules. In fact, the kidnapping later proved to be a Mafia plot.

It took the Mafia many months to convinced anyone that Getty had been kidnapped. The youth was chained most of the time, but his captors gave him plenty of booze and some watercolor paints to play with. Eventually, about October 21, 1973, they gave Getty a haircut and a steak for dinner. When he finished eating they put a handkerchief in his mouth, told him to bite down hard, and then they cut off his right ear. A few days later they took a picture of his head, sans ear.

The ear was mailed to a Rome newspaper. It was delayed by a postal strike, but when found at last it convinced many doubters. The picture then arrived and it convinced the remainder. Moreover, the ear conveyed the threat that other bits of the boy's body—fingers, toes, eyes—might be sent if additional identification was needed.

It wasn't—almost three billion lire, worth 2.9 million American dollars, weighing a ton, was delivered in a truck to Calabria by agents of the Richest Man in The World. On December 15, 1973, young Getty was released. When he called his grandfather to thank him, the old man wouldn't talk to him lest the phone call itself might be a plot. Through an aide, however, he wished his grandson, "Good luck."

Grandfather Getty was an oil man and oil men weren't too popular in the United States

152

Eugene Paul Getty II with Italian
Carabinieri after his release from
five months and five days of captivity.
The boy's ear had been cut off by
his captors to show proof of his
kidnapping. His grandfather then paid
2.9 million American dollars for
his release.

Ear cut off but in reasonable health

ROME, Saturday. --- J. Paul Getty III, kidnapped grandson of the American oil multi-millionaire, was found alive by police on a highway in south Italy early today with his right ear cut off.

"I am Paul Getty, captain, give me a cigarette. Look, they have cut an ear," were words to the p which found h

The G

at that time. So while many people felt sorry that young Getty had lost his ear, few were disturbed at the prospect of old Getty losing almost three million dollars.

Much the same sentiment was expressed on December 6, 1973, when Victor E. Samuelson was kidnapped in Argentina. A refinery manager for the Exxon Corporation, Samuelson was seized by the "People's Revolutionary Army," a leftist guerilla group. The fact that he was the father of three small children back in Cleveland was somehow obscured when his company paid a $14.2 million ransom for his release. Public sentiment seemed to be that the oil company could afford it if anyone could.

By the time the ransom was paid in March 1974, so much had happened it was just another story. Forty-five more days passed before Samuelson was released, and by then he had been almost forgotten by the public.

What was clear, however, was that the Samuelson kidnapping was politically

motivated. While money was the object, the money was to be used to aid the revolution. Disturbing, but still only one of many exotic incidents south of the border where the natives were left to enjoy the "benign neglect" of the United States. Smugly, most Americans assumed there was no such revolutionary zeal loose in the States.

Then, on February 4, 1974, the young heiress Patricia Campbell Hearst was carried screaming from her apartment in Berkeley, California, and, suddenly, the Watergate story had competition.

It happened, as *Newsweek* put it, "with the explosive precision of a commando raid." At about 9 P.M. a white woman knocked on the door of the townhouse. Steven A. Weed, a Princeton graduate and Berkeley philosophy student, answered the knock. He lived there with Patricia, as openly though certainly not as flamboyantly as the girl's grandfather, William Randolph Hearst, had lived for decades with actress Marion Davies. Weed and

EXXON MANAGER YET TO BE FREED

Ransom of $14-Million Paid in Argentina but Guerrillas Still Hold American

Peronist leftists, ... ulty posts.

not own the Gov-

No Sign of Oilman in Argentina 4 Days After Ransom Payment

BUENOS AIRES, March 15 (AP)—The whereabouts of Victor Samuelson, the kidnapped American oil company executive ...

handed over a suitcase of 142,-000 $100 bills at a rendezvous with guerrillas.

The company had offered $7-million, but was told that Mr. ...

Yank's Condition OK After Kidnap

Cordoba, Argentina, April 13 (UPI)—An American diplomat who was shot, pistol-whipped and drugged during a brief kidnaping yesterday near this central Argentine city, rested in "satisfactory" condition today, according to a local hospital spokesman

The diplomat, Alfred A. Laun 3d, 36, of Kiel, Wis., was shot in the abdomen yesterday morning when he resisted guerrillas from the People's Revolutionary Army who dragged him from his breakfast table in his home in the suburbs of Cordoba, 400 miles northwest of Buenos Aires, police said.

fered in the beating." It also said its medical information indicated that he had been given psychedelic drugs by his captors.

The terrorists sent a clandestine communique to news media saying it "c...
of the ...
Alfre...

(Opposite page) An article relating to the kidnap of Victor E. Samuelson. Exxon paid over $14 million ransom.
(Left) Some news clips relating to the kidnapping.

(Left) Patricia Hearst and her fiancé, Steven Weed, twenty-six, shown in a 1973 photo.
(Above) The Berkeley, California, apartment where S.L.A. members burst in, attacked Weed and then forced the girl outside and into the trunk of a car. The S.L.A. fired a warning burst at the neighbors as they drove away.

157

Patricia were engaged and planned to marry.

For reasons not explained, Weed refused to allow the caller to use the telephone as she requested. Two black men then appeared with rifles and broke the door down. Weed, trying to resist, was beaten across the head. He broke free and ran—for help, he said.

Patricia, half-wrapped in a blue bathrobe, was carried out to the trunk of a waiting car. Witnesses agreed she was screaming, but the import of her screams was a matter of some dispute. She was stuffed in the trunk. The kidnappers fired a volley of shots, apparently designed to intimidate onlookers, and roared away. An old station wagon followed. Some eight blocks away they stopped, switched their captive to the station wagon, and disappeared. The abandoned car had been stolen earlier in the night along with its driver, Paul Benenson. During the kidnapping, Benenson had lain bound, gagged and terrified on the floor between the seats.

Three days passed as the nation speculated on the size of the probable ransom demand and read background stories about the Hearsts. Since Patricia's father was a publisher, most of the stories were favorable. At this point it was just another kidnapping—a major kidnapping, true, something more sensational than the Greenlease case, less spectacular than the Lindbergh. Then abruptly everything changed.

A letter came to radio station KFPA, San Francisco. Enclosed was an oil credit card issued to Randolph A. Hearst, but used by Patricia. The letter looked like this:

SYMBIONESE LIBERATION ARMY
Western Regional Adult Unit
Communique # 3   February 4, 1974
Subject: Prisoner of War
Target: Patricia Campbell Hearst
        Daughter of Randolph Hearst
        corporate enemy of the people

Warrant Order:
Arrest and protective custody; and if resistance, execution
Warrant Issued by: The Court of the People

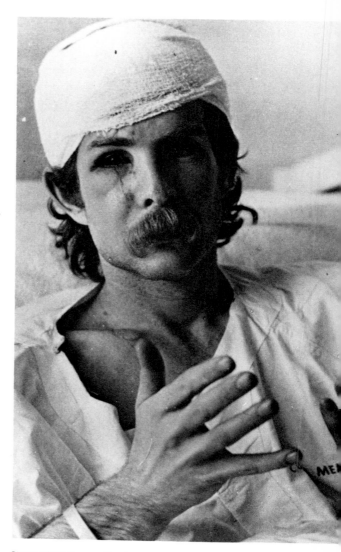

Steven Weed recuperating from injuries sustained during the kidnapping. "I felt my head was going to cave in," Weed said of his experience.

San Francisco Chronicle

The Largest Daily Circulation in Northern California

★★★★   **WEDNESDAY, FEBRUARY 6, 1974**   GArfield 1-1111   15 CENTS

Hearst Daughter Abducted
By 3 Armed 'Commandos'

**Kidnapers Burst Into
Berkeley Apartment--
Her Fiance Is Beaten**

**Kidnaped Girl's Fiance
Tells of Brutal Attack**

Hearst Heiress, 19, Kidnaped
Dad Radios Plea to Gunmen
After Blazing Getaway

By THEO WILSON

Terror Group Claims
It Has the Hearst Girl

DAILY NEWS, FRIDAY, FEBRUARY 8

Kidnapers: Try Rescue & She'll Die

Berkeley, Calif., Feb. 7 (Special)—The mysterious Symbionese Liberation Army said today that it had kidnaped Patricia Hearst and that the 19-year-old newspaper heiress was unharmed. But it threatened to execute her "should any attempt be made by authorities to rescue the prisoner . . ."

The group   itself as a multiracial revolutionary

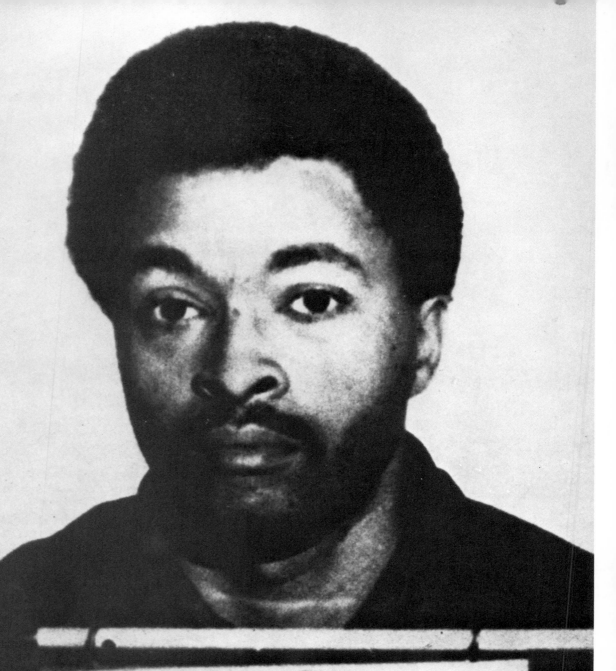

CALIFORNIA PRISON
B24833A
D D DE FREEZE
1   16   73

WANTED BY THE FBI

BANK ROBBERY
INTERSTATE FLIGHT – POSSESSION OF HOMEMADE BOMB, ...BERY, RECEIVING STOLEN PROPERTY, ASSAULT WITH FORCE

DONALD DAVID DE FREEZE

...ograph taken 1973   Date photographs taken unknown   FBI No. 606,723 D

Aliases: Don Cinque DeFreeze, Donald John DeFreeze, Donald DeFrez, John DeFriele, David DeFrieze, Donald DeFrieze, Donald DeFrize, David Kenneth Robinson, Steven Robinson, Donald David Thomas, "Cin," "Cinque," "Cynque"

DESCRIPTION

Age:	30, born November 16, 1943, Cleveland, Ohio	
Height:	5'9" to 5'11"	**Eyes:** Brown
Weight:	150 to 160 pounds	**Complexion:** Medium brown
Build:	Medium	**Race:** Negro
Hair:	Black	**Nationality:** American

Occupations: Autobody shop worker, carpenter, chef, painter, restaurant manager, service station attendant, stationary engineer, typist, key punch operator

Scars and Marks: Scar on bridge of nose, scars on forehead, face, left arm and wrist, right elbow and palm of right hand, appendectomy scar

Remarks: Reportedly drinks plum wine, may be wearing tinted glasses

Social Security Number Used: 042-34-4002

Fingerprint Classification: 9 S 1 R 1OI 12
S 1 U OOI

CRIMINAL RECORD

...Freeze has been convicted of robbery, possession of homemade bomb, possession of stolen property, ...ault with force, and forgery.

CAUTION

...FREEZE, AN ESCAPEE FROM A PENAL INSTITUTION, REPORTEDLY HAS HAD NUMEROUS ...REARMS IN HIS POSSESSION AND ALLEGEDLY HAS FIRED ON LAW ENFORCEMENT OFFICERS ... AVOID ARREST. DE FREEZE, WITH ACCOMPLICES, ALLEGEDLY ROBBED A BANK USING ...TOMATIC WEAPONS. TWO INDIVIDUALS WERE KNOWN TO HAVE BEEN SERIOUSLY WOUNDED ...RING SHOOTING AT THE BANK. DE FREEZE SHOULD BE CONSIDERED ARMED AND EX-...EMELY DANGEROUS.

...Federal warrant was issued on February 8, 1974, at Salinas, California, charging DeFreeze with ...awful interstate flight to avoid confinement after conviction for robbery, possession of homemade ...b, receiving stolen property, and assault with force (Title 18, U. S. Code, Section 1073). Also on ...il 16, 1974, a Federal warrant was issued at San Francisco, California, charging DeFreeze with bank ...bery (Title 18, U. S. Code, Sections 2113(a), (d)).

...YOU HAVE ANY INFORMATION CONCERNING THIS PERSON, PLEASE NOTIFY ME OR CONTACT YOUR ...AL FBI OFFICE. TELEPHONE NUMBERS AND ADDRESSES OF ALL FBI OFFICES LISTED ON BACK.

C. M. Kelley

DIRECTOR
FEDERAL BUREAU OF INVESTIGATION
UNITED STATES DEPARTMENT OF JUSTICE
WASHINGTON, D. C. 20535
TELEPHONE, NATIONAL 8-7117

...red NCIC
...ted Flyer 473
...il 17, 1974

(Opposite page) Donald DeFreeze's arrest photo.
(Left) His F.B.I. "Wanted" notice which outlined his complete criminal career.
(Above) Joseph Cinque, the slave after whom DeFreeze named himself.
(Below) The seven-headed cobra, symbol of the Symbionese Liberation Army.

(Above) Russell Little and Joseph Remiro are led away from the courthouse, after a Contra Costa county judge turned down their request to make a television appearance as demanded by the kidnappers of Patricia Hearst.
(Opposite page) Graffiti found on the wall of an abandoned hideout of the S.L.A.

On the above stated date, combat elements of the United Federated Forces of the Symbionese Liberation Army armed with cyanide loaded weapons served an arrest warrant upon Patricia Campbell Hearst. It is the order of this court that the subject be arrested by combat units and removed to a protective area of safety and only upon completion of this condition to notify Unit # 4 to give communication of this action. It is the directive of this court that during this action ONLY, no civilian elements be harmed if possible, and that warning shots be given. However, if any citizens attempt to aid the authorities or interfere with the implementation of this order, they shall be executed immediately. This court hereby notifies the public and directs all combat units in the future to shoot to kill any civilian who attempts to witness or interfere with any operation conducted by the peoples forces against the fascist state. Should any attempt be made by authorities to rescue the prisoner, or to arrest or harm any S.L.A. elements, the prisoner is to be executed. The prisoner is to be maintained in adequate physical and mental condition, and unharmed as long as these conditions are adhered to. Protective custody shall be composed of combat and medical units, to safeguard both the prisoner and her health. All communications from this court MUST be published in full, in all newspapers, and all other forms of the media. Failure to do so will endanger the safety of the prisoner. Further communications will follow.

S.L.A.
DEATH TO THE FASCIST INSECT THAT PREYS UPON THE LIFE OF THE PEOPLE

The first questions were about the Symbionese Liberation Army. What was it? Where did it come from? What did it want? Information was scarce. The leader and founder appeared to be Donald David DeFreeze, a black thirty-year-old escaped convict. One of eight children in Cleveland, he had run away from home at the age of fourteen. He was constantly in trouble—in New York, New Jersey and, finally, California. Most of his arrests involved possession of guns and bombs. Once he was arrested for nothing

Patria O Muerte.
Venceremos.

Tania

Death to the FASCIST INSECT
THat preys upon the life
OF THE people!

more sinister than running a red light on a bicycle. But then in the bicycle's basket a bomb was found.

In 1969, he was sentenced to five years in a California prison. There he became "educated," picking up the ideology and the rhetoric he needed to clothe his rebellion in revolutionary dress. He formed a study group and invited white radicals from outside the prison to join. And he adopted the "reborn" African name "Cinque Mitume."

Plans completed, he escaped from prison in March 1973, and began to implement them. Oakland became his headquarters and there the S.L.A. was born. It apparently consisted of a strange group of upper middle-class whites— many of them women—and some Vietnam veterans. The "soldiers" swore to follow "black and minority" leadership. Cinque adopted the rank of "Field Marshal." Marriage, monogamy and male chauvinism as well as racism, sexism, ageism, capitalism, fascism and individualism would be abolished in the brave, new world

they planned to create upon the ruins of the corporate state.

On November 6, 1973, the S.L.A. made its debut by murdering Marcus Foster, the black school superintendent of Oakland. He was blasted with cyanide-tipped bullets, and "Communique # 1" explained that Foster had been killed because he supported a plan to have identification photographs made of Oakland students. Such a plan was part of a sinister scheme for an "Internal Warfare Identification Computer," the S.L.A. said.

Instead of rallying revolutionary-minded radicals to the cause, the killing seemed to have scared them off. So, at least, thought police. Nothing much was heard from the S.L.A. for two months. Then on January 10, 1974, police in the suburb of Concord stopped a battered Chevy van. The two men in it pulled pistols. One, Russell Little, was wounded and captured; Joseph Remiro escaped on foot but was captured four hours later within a block of the secret S.L.A.

163

Surrounded by newspersons, Mr. and
Mrs. Randolph Hearst at their
Hillsborough home. They had then
received a second tape-recorded
message from their nineteen-year-
old daughter.

headquarters. Police learned of the headquarters that evening when an attempt was made to burn it down. Firemen put out the blaze and discovered a bomb factory as well as books, records, and propaganda leaflets. BB shots had peppered the walls, apparently the result of target practice.

Several of the S.L.A. members were identified as a result of the evidence left behind, but all vanished. Among the items recovered by police was a green notebook which contained among other things this entry:

"Patricia Campbell Hearst on the night of the full moon of January 7."

Apparently the entry meant little to the police. Nothing was said about it until April. Obviously, a lot of officials were hoping the whole thing was a bad dream that might go away if steadfastly ignored. Another "communique" on February 12 only heightened the sense of the grotesque. This one was in the form of a tape-cassette and was delivered to the same radio station. "Field Marshal" Cinque gave terms for release of his prisoner: to show "repentance" the Hearsts

had to arrange to deliver $70 worth of "quality" food over the next four weeks to every Californian in need—roughly 5.9 million people. Such a program, it was estimated, could cost $400 million.

It was shocking and different, something new in the history of American kidnappings. As if to assure the Hearsts and the public that it was not a black joke of some kind, there was Patricia's voice on the tape—a tired, weary voice but recognizable. Reassuring her parents that she was all right, she asked them not to allow the police to attempt her rescue. "These people," said the girl, "aren't just a bunch of nuts. They're perfectly willing to die for what they're doing."

Hastily, Hearst organized a handout for the needy despite criticism from some that to accept food that was part of a ransom payment was to become an accessory after the fact. Governor Ronald Reagan suggested it would be well if all those eating the food developed botulism. Nevertheless, hundreds stood in line for hours at designated spots to receive two frozen turkey hindquarters, two 12-ounce cans

166

(Opposite page) A poster of the S.L.A.
symbol at the food distribution point
in San Francisco.
(Above) In Richmond, California, free
food is distributed in cartons by the
People In Need program established
by Randolph A. Hearst to gain release
of his daughter.

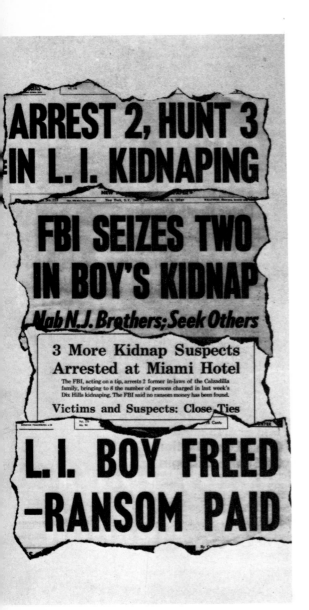

ARREST 2, HUNT 3 IN L. I. KIDNAPING

FBI SEIZES TWO IN BOY'S KIDNAP

Nab N.J. Brothers; Seek Others

3 More Kidnap Suspects Arrested at Miami Hotel

The FBI, acting on a tip, arrests 2 former in-laws of the Calzadilla family, bringing to 8 the number of persons charged in last week's Dix Hills kidnaping. The FBI said no ransom money has been found.

Victims and Suspects: Close Ties

L. I. BOY FREED —RANSOM PAID

of tomato juice, two cans of luncheon meat, and a box of saltine crackers. It wasn't exactly the "quality" food demanded by the SLA, but it was welcomed by mothers with children, unemployed workers, elderly pensioners. In East Oakland a riot began after a crowd of five thousand became restless and frightened clerks began tossing the food baskets to the crowd from trucks as if feeding wild animals.

The S.L.A. had scored a propaganda victory in dramatizing the reality of hunger. And when it complained about the quality of the food given away, Hearst promised to improve it.

And then the inevitable happened. In Atlanta, the editor of the *Constitution,* Reg Murphy, was kidnapped by a man claiming to represent "the American Revolutionary Army." The A.R.A. was the right-wing counterpart of the S.L.A., Murphy was told, and among other things it wanted all federal officials to resign so that free elections could be held. Meanwhile, it would settle for a $700,000 ransom.

The newspaper put up the money, the drop was made by Managing Editor Jim Minter and Murphy was released. A few hours later the F.B.I. arrested William A.H. Williams and his wife, Betty, in their home at Lilburn, Georgia, and recovered the money. The A.R.A., Williams admitted, was something he had dreamed up after reading about the S.L.A.

Then on March 6, an eight-year-old boy, John Calzadilla, was kidnapped on Long Island while walking home from school. His father, a tire-company executive, paid a $50,000 ransom, and two days later John walked into a Holiday Inn in New Jersey, ordered a Coke with some change given him by the kidnappers, and tried to call home. Bystanders agreed that the boy was "real cool" about it. Less than twenty-four hours later the F.B.I. seized two Cuban refugee brothers in Union City, New Jersey, and charged them with the crime. Three more ex-Cubans were arrested in Miami a few days later. The

(Above) Shattered glass litters the road around the royal limousine after a gunman fired shots at Princess Anne and her husband as they traveled toward Buckingham Palace.

The white Ford (below) was used by the lone gunman, Ian Ball. He fired six shots into the royal limousine and wounded the chauffeur, a bodyguard, a policeman and a newsman. Ball was arrested at the scene of the crime.

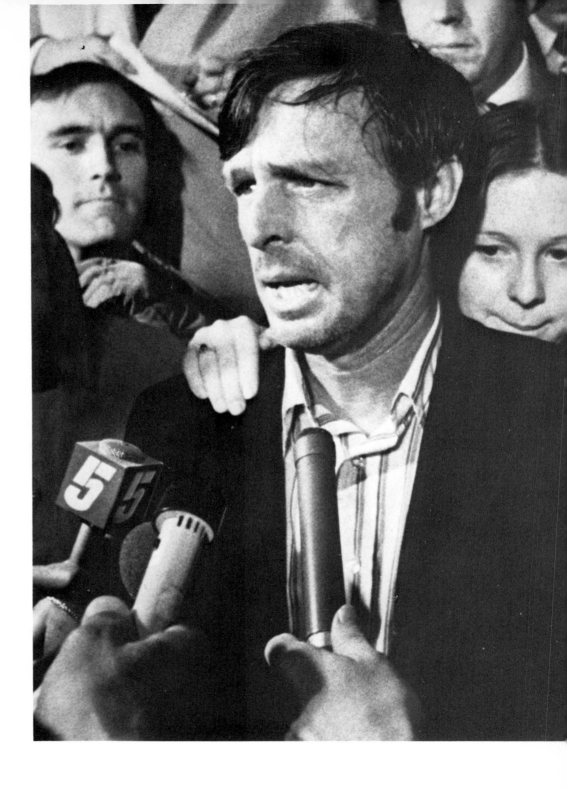

(Above left) *Atlanta Constitution* editor Reg Murphy, freed on February 2, 1974, by kidnappers for $700,000 ransom. Beside Murphy are (left to right) his daughters Karen, seventeen, Susan, thirteen, and his wife Virginia.

(Top right) His kidnappers in custody, Mrs. Betty Ruth Williams and William Halm Williams.

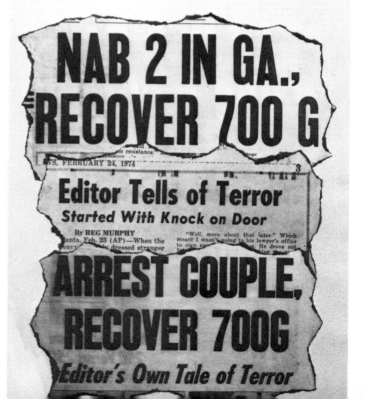

NAB 2 IN GA., RECOVER 700 G

VS. FEBRUARY 24, 1974   3

Editor Tells of Terror
Started With Knock on Door

By REG MURPHY

anta, Feb. 23 (AP)—When the eavy ... dressed stranger

"Well, more about that later." Which meant I wasn't going to his lawyer's office to sign ... s. He drove out

ARREST COUPLE, RECOVER 700G

Editor's Own Tale of Terror

ransom money got away, however, at least temporarily.

Minneapolis, scene of the famous kidnappings of the 1930's, took the spotlight briefly on March 15. Mrs. Gunnar Kronholm, the wife of a bank president, was seized while scraping the ice from her car window. Her husband paid $200,000 for her release. When one member of the team was arrested, the other became frightened and allowed her to walk away after four days. All but $10,000 of the ransom was recovered.

The big sensation came on the night of March 20. England's Princess Anne and her new husband were driving down London's Mall toward Buckingham Palace after viewing a film about horseback riding. Suddenly, a little white Ford zipped in front of the royal car, forcing it to stop.

A man jumped out of the Ford and fired a volley of shots at the royal bodyguard, who was hit in the chest, arm and shoulder. The chauffeur was also shot—in the stomach. Reaching the door of the royal car, the gunman tried to open it. Captain Mark Phillips, Anne's husband, held tightly to the door as Anne screamed: "Get away, get away."

Baffled, the attacker tried to run around the rear of the royal car. A reporter leaped out of a taxi to stop him, and fell wounded to the pavement. A policeman came rushing up and was shot in the stomach. The gunman tried to get in the other side, firing wildly in his frustration. One bullet missed the Princess by inches.

Giving up, the would-be kidnapper fled into St. James's Park where another policeman, Peter Edmonds, tackled him. Meanwhile, Samantha Scott, a yoga teacher, rushed up to the royal car and looked inside.

"Are you all right, luv?" she asked.

"I'm fine," replied Anne. "Thank you."

An undelivered ransom note was found in the white Ford. It demanded $4.6 million in "reparation" for blacks, workers, victims of inflation and of the Irish conflict. Its author,

SPANIARDS SEARCH WOMEN ON AMERICAN STEAMER

(Opposite page, top) William Randolph
Hearst and his *Journal* fanned the
flames of war with blatant yellow
journalism such as the drawing
(opposite page below) by Frederic
Remington that purported that American
women were searched by Spanish men
on ships. The male searchers were
only in the mind of Richard
Harding Davis.
But once started, anti-Spanish feeling
ran high everywhere. Other editorial
cartoons of the day: (above) the great
spark starting the Spanish-American
War, the explosion of the battleship
Maine, and (below) the sentiments
it engendered.

(Above) Under heavy security
protection, Ian Ball, twenty-six, is
led in handcuffs to court where he was
charged with the attempted murder of
Princess Anne's bodyguard after he
failed in a kidnap attempt on
the Princess.
(Opposite page, top) Princess Anne
visits her personal bodyguard,
Inspector James Beaton, at the
hospital. She also visited the others
wounded in the kidnap attempt.

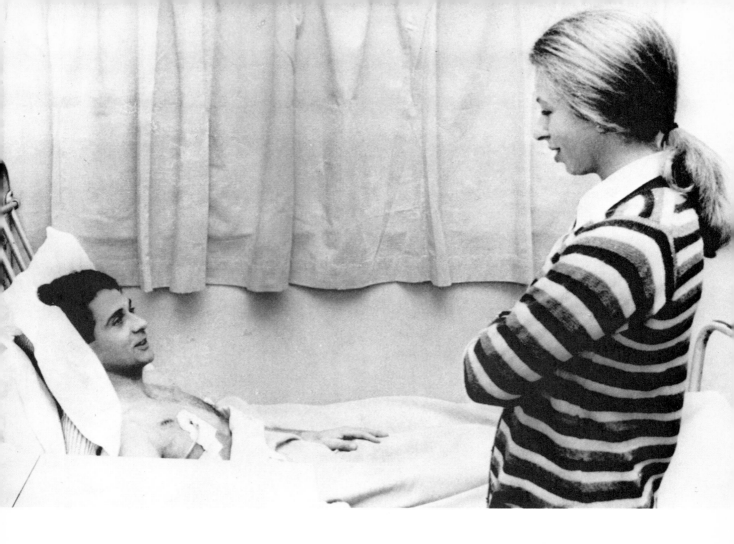

MARCH 21, 19__

Princess Anne and Her Husband Escape Kidnapping Attempt as Car Is Fired On

achine gun attack on royal couple

4 Hurt in Attack Near Palace —Suspect Detained at Scene

By ALVIN SHUSTER
Special to The New York Times

ANNE ESCAPES

__DON, March 20 — A__ and trying to get in," one wit-
__fired several shots to-__ness said.
__a car carrying__
__nne and her hus__ __tness reported that
__k Phill__

__N, Wednesday (Reuter) - Britain's Princess Anne
__ husband Captain Mark Phillips tonight escaped
__assination attempt by a gunman who forced her
__car to a halt near Buckingham Palace and opened
__ kidnap attempt.

chauffeur, were wounded in what at first appeared to be
a bid to assassinate the Royal couple.
    But later Home Secretary Roy Jenkins told a shocked
Parliament that the incident was part of an abortive
kidnap plot.

__ Scotland Yard__ut a
__spoke__n for the North

__TO wants reduction
start with U.S. and Soviet
troops in Central Europe.

__ase" for __
trade commitments, but __
not require Senate confirmation

Anne's Attacker Is Committed

By HENRY MAULE
Staff Correspondent of The News

London, May 22—Ian Ball, a 26-year-old unemployed truck driver, was committed to a mental hospital
today "without limit of time" for atte__

the gunman, was identified as Ian Ball, a twenty-six-year-old loner. When captured he had three pairs of handcuffs, some tranquilizers, and $700 in cash. Apparently he was trying to be a one-man gang. Neighbors said he was "shy."

The Economist, one of England's leading publications, noted editorially:

Crime of this kind is imitative: it may be that it was not so much the royalty of Princess Anne that made her a target as the fact that she is the daughter of a rich woman. The kidnapping of Mr. Randolph Hearst's daughter and of Mr. Paul Getty's grandson have been much in the news. It would not be at all reassuring if that were what exercised the mind of the Princess's attacker, but it would make the incident more explicable.

Perhaps. But if Anne's adventure could be easily explained, the same could not be said of the Patty Hearst case. That headline writers and public officials now spoke of her as Patty instead of Patricia or Miss Hearst was in itself indicative of the changing status of the kidnap victim. For Patty was not maintaining her dignity. The day after the value of food given away by Hearst passed the one million dollar mark, the S.L.A. broke a long silence with another tape recording. One of the speakers was Patty. In a soft but steady voice she accused her father of not doing his best. Had he obeyed the S.L.A.'s original demand, she said, "I would be out of here."

Other remarks by Patty seemed so untypical that for the first time speculation began that the entire kidnapping episode was a hoax, that Patty was in league with her kidnappers. This was emphatically denied by her fiancé and indignantly rejected by her parents, yet a more searching examination of the girl and her background was made by various observers.

It had all begun with George Hearst, a rough, tough, illiterate who discovered a mountain of silver in California in the 1850's and became a respected pioneer. At age forty-two, he went home to Missouri and

(Above) Revolutionary material readily available in many bookstores, some of which gives detailed instructions on the making of explosives.
(Right) A photo of Tania (née Patty Hearst) received April 3 by radio station KSAN, San Francisco. She stands armed with automatic weapon in front of a Symbionese Liberation Army banner. The message received with this picture declared that she had joined the S.L.A.

The automatic camera pictures taken
of the band that robbed the Hibernia
Bank on April 15, 1974. (Left) Donald
De Freeze. (Top, left to right) Patricia
''Mizmoon'' Soltysik, Nancy Ling Perry
and Camilla Christine Hall. (Below)
A general view of the bank interior
with Patty Hearst at center, apparently
under duress from the presence of
guns on either side.
(Above) The exterior of the
Hibernia Bank.

(Continued on page 32, col. 1)

Cinque Sought As Leader of 'Army' Heist

San Francisco, April 16 (Special) — Donald David DeFreeze, the mysterious General field Cinque o...

Was Patty Forced to Play Bank Robber?

By ALTON SLAGLE

Is she or isn't she? The theories fly thick and fast. You can believe almost anything now about Patricia Campbell Hearst and back it with a strong argument. Her story is that bizarre. But is the newspaper heiress now a revolutionary?

Regardless of whether Patty Hearst entered the Hibernia Bank in San Francisco on Monday as Tania, the revolutionary name she may or may not have adopted voluntarily, or as Patricia Hearst, unwilling victim, the fact remains that her comrades, or captors, took a great chance in staging the robbery.

It seemed evident to many on April 3—when, in a message from the Symbionese Liberation Army, Miss Hearst renounced her parents and vowed to fight alongside the guerrilla band—that she had been coerced, brainwashed, during two months of captivity.

'We Had Her 20 Years'

Her parents, Randolph and Catherine Hearst; her fiance, Steven Weed; the FBI, and others close to Patty refused to believe that she had changed her political philosophy so drastically and so rapidly. "We had...

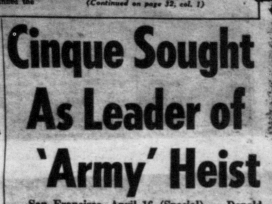

Photograph taken by bank camera during robbery shows armed woman, in center, identified as Patricia Hearst. At far left and right are suspects armed with similar weapons.

DAILY NEWS, TUESDAY, APRIL 16, 1974

Tie Pat Hearst to Bank Holdup
Say Photos Show Her With Gun

...o, April 15 (AP) — New...

Hearst Says Patty Isn't Linked to SLA

Another automatic camera picture taken at the Hibernia Bank. (Left) Patty Hearst, weapon in hand. (Above) News clips of the incident.

From Combined Services

HILLSBOROUGH, Cal. —Randolph Hearst says he doesn't "see any reason to believe" that his kidnapped daughter was involved with or knew about the ...

"I think all the kids are against discrimination, for one thing. I think all the kids today are... are, and should be... fed up with the racial so-called problems we have. ... part of the nor...

versity, any school in the country.

"But I don't think she's said anything that was all that radical, what she said was that... she was afraid [the FBI] was going to come out and shoot her...

181

married a girl half his age, a schoolteacher. They moved into a mansion on Nob Hill, overlooking San Francisco, and there in 1863 the legendary William Randolph Hearst, Patty's grandfather, was born.

With his father's wealth and his own genuis, William Randolph Hearst built up a newspaper empire that liberals assailed for generations. But the man was more than a publisher—he was, in his own way, a reformer who sought to use the press as a tool to attain political power. The Spanish-American War was largely his invention, a necessary step, he thought, if America was to achieve its destiny. At one time he seriously considered running for President, but he enjoyed the role of king-maker too much to venture far from the shadows.

He was a married man with five sons when he fell in love with Marion Davies, a New York show girl. To make her a star, he bought a movie studio and eventually moved to California to live with her apart from his wife, Millicent, who steadfastly refused to give him

a divorce. For Marion he built a fantastic castle by the ocean called San Simeon. It had two nippled towers and more than one hundred rooms. In those rooms he placed the art treasures of Europe. His personal suite had gold-plated bathroom fixtures and a bed once owned by Cardinal Richelieu. On the studio lot of M.G.M., he built a fourteen-room bungalow for Marion, and put a statue of the madonna above the door.

His five sons by his wife Millicent were George, fat and fun-loving, who died in 1972; William Jr., who became editorial spokesman for the Hearst newspapers after the death of columnist Arthur Brisbane; John, who died in 1949; and the fraternal twins, Randolph and David, born before their father met Miss Davies at the *Follies of 1917*.

Because of the marital triangle, the twins grew up in New York under the care of their mother. Their summers were spent with their father at San Simeon. Randy went on to prep school and to Harvard. He was "invited" to leave Harvard, however, when a girl was found

(Far Left) Pedro De Cordoba, Marion Davies and Young Diana, 1922.
(Left) Marion Davies in 1920.

in his room. Like his brothers he went to work to learn the newspaper business. There were thirty some newspapers in the Hearst empire, plus magazines and radio stations. Each son could find a place.

"Randy," as he was commonly called, went to work on the now dead *Georgian,* and promptly married a Southern belle—only after his father had private detectives ascertain the status of her family. Five daughters were born to them, of whom Patty was the third.

The Hearst empire suffered financial losses as the years went by and was on the verge of bankruptcy when its founder died in 1951. One by one his newspapers died too, until, in 1974, only eight remained. But while power and influence fell off sharply, there was plenty of money.

Patty Hearst grew up in a twenty-two room mansion in Hillsborough, a wealthy suburb of San Francisco. There were nurses and servants and a sense of well-being even if it did not include a very clear understanding of family history. Patty had never seen *Citizen Kane,*

the classic movie Orson Wells made about her grandfather, nor had she read *Citizen Hearst,* the biography by W.A. Swanberg. A friend who knew her well called her "sheltered and naïve, a blank slate."

Five feet, two inches tall, Patty had long brown hair, blue eyes, lovely skin, and a good mind. Her grades had been average at Menlo College until she became romantically involved with Weed, six years her senior. Suddenly motivated, she graduated first in her class and went on to study art history at Berkeley where Weed was a graduate student in philosophy. According to published reports, he introduced her to marijuana and psychedelic drugs, and she moved in with him. With an allowance of $300 a month and the use of her father's credit cards, she was able to give the apartment they shared "a veneer of elegance." While she had ducked some of the responsibilities of upper-class maidenhood—she had refused to make a formal debut, for one thing—there was every indication that she planned after marriage to settle down to a sedate existence.

(Opposite page, top) Nile Dwane Marx
and his wife Shirley, arrested
February 19 on charges of
impersonating the kidnappers of
Patricia Hearst. They had attempted
to collect $100,000 in ransom and
were arrested as they attempted to
collect the money.
(Opposite page, below) Ralph Lee
Jones is led into the Federal
courthouse for arraignment. He had
allegedly mailed three letters to the
Randolph Hearst family claiming to
know the whereabouts of Patricia and
demanded $100,000 for the information.
The crime carries a five year to
life sentence.
(Above) Newsmen listen to the latest
tape from the S.L.A. delivered
March 11 to radio station KSAN in
San Francisco.

Her wardrobe in the apartment consisted of one good wool dress, one long skirt, two cotton dresses, three pairs of good pants, six pairs of blue jeans, and some sweaters and T-shirts. Yet much of her time just prior to the kidnapping was spent shopping for silver, china and crystal as a girl might do who soon expected to become a formal hostess.

A person such as Patty Hearst appeared to be, according to those who knew her best, would hardly have been a conspirator associated with hard-core revolutionaries to pull a gigantic hoax on the public and bring sorrow to her bland and uncomprehending parents. But—there was reportedly the "blank slate," her inexperienced and untried mind.

Some experts maintain that a female kidnap victim experiences a love-hate relationship with her male captor, if, of course, he mixes some concern for her well being along with his determination to gain his ends. In that connection, the case of Barbara Mackle offers some confirmation. Although Ruth, the kidnapper's girl friend, was kind to Barbara before she was buried in the box, Barbara emerged from the experience disliking her. Barbara has written: "I guess I have more feeling for Krist than Ruth. I've been told not to say this, but it is true."

Hearst, of course, a newspaper publisher who admittedly had never heard of A.J. Liebling, for many years the press's chief critic, could not accept either possibility—that his daughter had been a conspirator from the beginning or had been won over after her kidnapping. In his quiet, ordered existence, such things were impossible. Revolution was something your editors worried about; it had no personal relationship to the Hearst family. Asked about the possibility on March 11, 1974, he replied:

"I just don't believe it."

In an effort to satisfy his daughter and the S.L.A., however, Hearst revised the food-giveaway program to include steaks, frozen fish, chicken and turkey along with fresh fruit and milk. On March 25, thousands

A sheriff's patrol car goes by Mel's Sporting Goods store(above), site of a holdup by S.L.A. members, one of whom was allegedly Patty Hearst. A bullet hole is pointed out (right) which was made during the robbery.

lined up in the rain to receive the boxes that carried a reported supermarket value of $25 each.

The handout represented the last of the $2 million Hearst raised to finance the program. He announced, however, that an additional $4 million would be furnished by the Hearst Foundation and kept in escrow until his daughter was released.

Reaction was long in coming, but on April 2, a dozen long-stemmed American Beauty roses were delivered to a San Francisco underground newspaper. Attached was a communique from the S.L.A. and one half of Patty's driver's license. The communique was principally concerned with a "code of war" which it demanded all newspapers publish. But it ended on a hopeful note:

"Further communications regarding subject will follow in the following 72 hours. Communications will state the state, city and time of the release of the prisoner."

As to underscore the hard line the F.B.I. would follow once Patty was free, Attorney General William B. Saxbe declared in Washington that the Hearst kidnappers followed instructions in a terrorist handbook. He called the use of the book evidence of "a world-wide conspiracy." The right-wing press applauded.

Next day the roof fell in.

Another tape-recorded message was delivered to Radio Station KFTA. The message was from Patty Hearst. It began:

"I have never been forced to say anything on any tape. Nor have I been brainwashed, tortured, hypnotized or in any way confused."

She continued with a message for her parents, accusing her father of bad faith in the conduct of his food giveaway and saying her mother's acceptance of a second term appointment as a University of California Regent endangered her life.

"Your actions have taught me a lesson," she said, "and in a strange kind of way, I'm grateful to you."

Police officers carry Christine Johnson,
who fled from her burning home where
six S.L.A. members were later killed.
"I passed right by DeFreeze, he
could have killed me if he wanted to,"
she said in an interview.

Next was her fiancé—and the rapier was
quickly bloodied:

"We both know what really came down that
Monday night, but you don't know what's
happened since then. I have changed—grown.
I've become conscious and can never go back
to the life we led before. What I am saying
may seem cold to you and to my old friends,
but love doesn't mean the same thing to me
anymore.

"My love has expanded as a result of my
experiences to embrace all people. It's grown
into an unselfish love for my comrades here, in
prison and on the streets. A love that comes
from the knowledge that 'no one is free until
we all are free.' While I wished that you could
be a comrade, I don't expect it—all I expect is

that you try to understand the changes I've
gone through."

And now she applied the crusher:

"I have been given the choice of (1) being
released in a safe area, or (2) joining the forces
of the Symbionese Liberation Army and
fighting for my freedom and the freedom of all
oppressed people. I have chosen to stay and
fight."

Then followed a long exposition about the
"corporate state" and the manner in which it
abused power. Near the end she mentioned her
new identity:

"I have been given the name Tania after a
comrade who fought alongside Che (Guevara)
in Bolivia for the people of Bolivia. I embrace
the name with the determination to continue

188

Los Angeles Police Sergeant Charles
Loust points to a chart of the home in
which six members of the S.L.A. died.
Shown on the table in the foreground
are the weapons found in the rubble.
(Left to right) Four 30 caliber
automatic machine guns, six 12 gauge
shotguns, six handguns, and
two pipe bombs.

A mother flees, herding her children to safety in the adjoining house, as a police officer moves forward during shootout with six S.L.A. members.

DAILY NEWS, SATURDAY, MAY 18, 1974

5 Symbionese Slain in Raid
Report DeFreeze & Top Gal Among Dead in Fiery Raid

Los Angeles, May 17 (Special)—Police tonight killed five suspected members of the Symbionese Liberation Army in a blazing hour-long gun battle.

In a scene reminiscent of the fire fights in Europe during World War II or Vietnam, a police officer carrying a submachine gun runs into position to protect firemen as the house used by the S.L.A. crumbles.

The six members of the S.L.A. who perished in the blazing gun battle in Los Angeles. Tania Hearst described them in a new way in a headline-making message sent to station KPFA on June 7, 1974. In her words: (left to right, top row), Donald DeFreeze, "Cinque," ". . . loved people with tenderness and respect. He taught me . . . everything imaginable . . ." Patricia Soltysik, "Zoya," told Tania to ". . . keep her ass down and be bad . . ."
(Second row) Angela Atwood, "Gabi," was remembered ". . . crouched low with her ass to the ground with a shotgun, an extension of her right and left arms . . ." The big surprise was William Wolfe, or "Cujo," of whom Tania said, "Unconquerable. It was the perfect name for him . . . Neither Cujo nor I ever loved an individual the way we loved each other."
Nancy Ling Perry, "Fahiza," was ". . . a beautiful sister who was a teacher of many by her righteous example . . . who taught me to shoot first and make sure the pig was dead before splitting."
(Bottom) Camilla Hall, "Gelina," was ". . . beautiful, fire and joy . . ." She ". . . exploded with the desire to kill pigs . . ."

194

fighting with her spirit. There is no victory
in the half-assed attempts at revolution. I
know Tania dedicated her life to the people.
Fighting with total dedication and an intense
desire to learn which I will continue in the
oppressed people's revolution. All colors of
string in the web of humanity yearn for
freedom."

She concluded: "Patria O Muerte,
Venceremos," which means:

"Fatherland or Death, we shall overcome."

Informed of the message, Randolph A.
Hearst responded, said the *New York Times,*
"with a series of wordless moans."

Along with the message was a photograph
of "Tania" Hearst holding a submachine gun
at the ready. She seemed dressed in a uniform
of sorts and stood before a huge imprint of
a seven-headed cobra—the symbol of the
S.L.A.

The message seemed plain enough, but no
one wanted to believe it. Mrs. Hearst
commented the next day:

"Only Patty in person can convince me that
the terrible weary words came from her heart
and were delivered of her own free will."

The United States Attorney handling the
case put it more simply:

"I don't believe it," he said.

In Washington, Clarence M. Kelly, new
director of the F.B.I., said cautiously:

"The welfare and safety of Miss Hearst will
remain primary concerns of all F.B.I.
personnel as they have been from the outset."

Spokesmen for radical groups were quoted
as saying they believed Patty was dead—that
the tape had been made under duress before
she was killed.

And so the doubts and disbelief grew.
People who would never think to question the
integrity of tapes held by a politician fighting
for his political life, nevertheless were
convinced that Patty's tape had been doctored
to produce her long message.

Why?

Patty's defection, if defection it was,

A wreath placed by an unknown person
in memory of the six slain S.L.A.
members a few days after the shootout.

195

The casket of Donald DeFreeze, "General Field Marshall Cinque" of the Symbionese Liberation Army, is carried from the funeral home in Cleveland, Ohio. His brother (center) headed the entourage of one thousand lining the streets and driveway leading to the funeral home.

threatened too many comfortable illusions. Accepted at face value, a lot of things could no longer be regarded as certain. Words, however eloquent, would not convince.

So Patty went out and robbed a bank.

It was for many as shocking as the fall from power of Spiro Agnew.

One man and four women, their automatic weapons concealed beneath long coats, strolled into the Hibernia Bank's Sunset District branch on April 15 and robbed it of $10,900. The bank's hidden cameras made hundreds of pictures of the unmasked robbers. Slightly out of focus but easily recognizable was Patty Hearst.

According to witnesses she held a long gun at the ready and used harsh language to command obedience.

The single man among the robbers was identified as Donald D. DeFreeze, the self-proclaimed Field Marshal Cinque. It was DeFreeze who fired a burst from his weapon upon leaving the bank, wounding two innocent bystanders. The shots recalled those fired the night Patty was taken and apparently represented a signature in lead.

Again there was doubt. A warrant charging Patty Hearst with being a "material witness" to the bank robbery was issued, but the FBI refused to acknowledge her as a willing participant. Some of the pictures, said the F.B.I., showed S.L.A. members pointing a gun at Patty during the robbery. This raised the possibility, according to the F.B.I., that she had been forced to take part in the raid.

The Hearst family and its friends leaped desperately at this straw, hoping against hope that it might be true. When Attorney General Saxbe sounded off in dissent, calling Patty a "common criminal," he was rebuked by the Hearsts and various newspapers. It was one thing to blame the S.L.A. on a world-wide conspiracy, but something else to suggest that William Randolph Hearst's granddaughter was a part of it.

(Opposite page) Emily and William Taylor Harris, now underground with Patty Hearst.
(Above top) William Walls, eighty-three-year-old retired Army master sergeant, says that he talked with Patty Hearst and the Harrises when they asked for a night's lodging.
(Below) Tom Dean Mathews, eighteen-year-old youth allegedly kidnapped by Patty Hearst and the Harrises. They have been charged with his abduction.

Pete Hamill, writing in the *New York Post*, summed up the situation in an April 19 column:

We live in a whirlwind of absurdity, the top of the government a shambling pile of corruption, American mastery of the world's economy rapidly passing to Arabia, a sense that the whole system is rapidly becoming unraveled. Patricia Hearst an armed revolutionary? What is the surprise? This is a country in which William Calley yesterday moved toward early parole after being convicted of 22 homicides. He is 21 ahead of the S.L.A.

She was a girl of wealth and education, brought up in the sheltered atmosphere of a powerful dynasty, but she also often criticized her family—that such a girl should embrace a cause after being exposed to it is, as Hamill says, not really surprising. It would be surprising only if such a person rejected a chance to give her life meaning and purpose. One might even be considered fortunate in this age of crumbling values to find a cause to espouse.

Many questions remain unanswered at this writing. The saga of Tania Hearst is far from over. She may find the life of a guerrilla too demanding and decide to return to her old life. But at this point it seems that the young woman has heeded the logic of Carlos Marighela in that guerrilla handbook Saxbe found so sinister:

"The duty of a Revolutionary is to make the revolution."

Six S.L.A. members are dead, annihilated in a grisly holocast in Los Angeles. Patty, or, rather, Tania, is reputed to be in hiding and probably traveling with Emily and William Harris, the only known surviving S.L.A. members. Whether these three will suffer as dramatic, public, and crushing a defeat as their six compatriots did remains to be seen.

If nothing else, the kidnapping business has suffered a severe shock. The Hearst affair may have brought the ancient profession into such disrepute as to discourage free enterprise in this area for the foreseeable future.

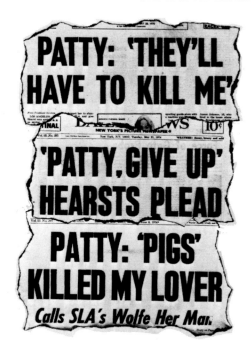

PICTURE CREDITS

ACKNOWLEDGMENTS

We appreciate the cooperation of the following people who have aided in the production of this book. The Columbia University Library and Jack Noordhoorn, The New York Public Library staff, Tayeb Jafferji, Warren and Ann Wallerstein, Paulette Nenner, Leslie Goldblatt who aided greatly in production, John Nordhaus, Isabel Rado, John Powers, the staff of Adams Photoprint Company, and for editorial assistance, Pat Meehan.

INDEX